Lunar Solo: Selected Poems

Jules Laforgue

Translated by Mark Ford

The Song Cave

The Song Cave
www.the-song-cave.com

Cover image: *Boy Blowing Soap Bubbles*, Édouard Manet, etching, 1868.

Design and layout by Janet Evans-Scanlon

ISBN: 979-8-9878288-2-3
Library of Congress Control Number: 2023948074

FIRST PRINTING

Contents

Introduction

In an article entitled "Reflections on Contemporary Poetry" published in *The Egoist* in July of 1919, T.S. Eliot mused in ardent but cryptic terms about an *amour fou* that had overwhelmed him some ten years earlier. The idol in question had excited in him a sense of "profound kinship," of "peculiar personal intimacy" so intense that he came to feel that he "alone" was the loved one's friend, that he "alone" possessed "secret knowledge" of the loved one's inner life. The "crisis" that resulted from this infatuation utterly transformed the nascent poet, for in the grip of this "imperative intimacy" Eliot found himself metamorphosed from "a bundle of second-hand sentiments into a person." A "first passion" of this kind, he continues, "arouses for the first time a real, an unshakeable confidence," and the consequent ability to "penetrate" (to use his own term) the object of his affections is registered as all-transfiguring: "It is a cause of development, like personal relations in life. Like personal intimacies in life, it may and probably will pass, but it will be ineffaceable."

Although Eliot refrains from disclosing in this particular essay the identity of the poet with whom he shared his first "genuine affair," it is clear that he is recounting the thrill of his discovery of Jules Laforgue, whose work he initially encountered in A.J. Symons's *The Symbolist Movement in Literature* (1900). The metaphors used in "Reflections on

Contemporary Poetry" suggest the experience verged for Eliot on both the erotic and the miraculous, for it "changed" and "quickened" him, as if he too had been penetrated and fertilized, left, like an expectant mother, nurturing a "literary embryo." And time and again over the ensuing years Eliot singled out the French poet as the one who had decisively initiated him into the complex and adult mysteries of composition:

> When I discovered Jules Laforgue he gave me the same revelation which I imagine he has given to other people before and since; that is, he showed how much more use poetry could make of contemporary ideas and feelings, of the emotional quality of contemporary ideas, than one had supposed. ("Modern Tendencies in Poetry" (1920))

> Of Jules Laforgue, I can say that he was the first to teach me how to speak, to teach me the poetic possibilities of my own idiom of speech. ("What Dante Means to Me" (1950))

Despite such frequent name-checks, in the event Eliot never got around to devoting a stand-alone critical essay to his first love and primary early influence, an omission somewhat ruefully acknowledged towards the end of his life: "I have written about Baudelaire, but nothing about Jules Laforgue, to whom I owe more than to any one poet in any language." (This is from "To Criticize the Critic" of 1961.) The Laforguian, however, runs through Eliot's early poetry as insistently as writing through a stick of Brighton rock, and it is possible that he realized no critical exposition could ever match the dazzling homage displayed in poems such as "The Love Song of J. Alfred Prufrock" or "Rhapsody on a Windy Night."

Anyone, therefore, who has read Eliot's first collection, *Prufrock and Other Observations* of 1917, will have been inducted, without actually knowing it, into Laforgue's poetic techniques and idiom, and will find familiar the various "lunar incantations," to use an especially Laforguian phrase from "Rhapsody on a Windy Night," orchestrated by Laforgue's multifaceted ironies and quicksilver wit. Eliot's enormous debt became more difficult still to ignore after *Inventions of the March Hare*, a notebook containing drafts of poems composed between 1909 and 1917, was published in 1996; these early "inventions" vividly illustrate the extent to which the French poet taught Eliot "how to speak," for sequences such as "Mandarins" or "Goldfish" or "Suite Clownesque" are effectively variations extemporised on Laforgue's keyboard, and often verge on pastiche. The same, indeed, could be said of "Conversation Galante," which *was* included in Eliot's first volume, and whose final line, "Are we then so serious?," is a transposition of the close of Laforgue's "Autre Complainte de Lord Pierrot": "*C'était donc sérieux?*"

The ever-fluctuating quotients of seriousness and mockery in Laforgue's poetic universe—as in that of early Eliot—are not at all easy to pin down. A memorable paragraph in Symons's study conveys the extreme self-consciousness that plagues his speakers:

> It is an art of the nerves, this art of Laforgue, and it is what all art would tend towards if we followed our nerves on all their journeys. There is in it all the restlessness of modern life, the haste to escape from whatever weighs too heavily on the liberty of the moment, that capricious liberty which demands only room enough to hurry itself weary. It is distressingly conscious of the unhappiness of mortality, but it plays, somewhat uneasily, at a disdainful indifference. And it is out

> of these elements of caprice, fear, contempt, linked together by an embracing laughter, that it makes its existence.

Such a diagnosis might just as well be applied to Eliot's Prufrock, who exclaims in self-mocking distress, "It is impossible to say just what I mean! / But as if a magic lantern threw the nerves in patterns on a screen . . ."

The magnificent L'Âge d'Homme edition of Laforgue's *Œuvres Complètes* (1986-2000) runs to over 3,000 pages, and includes his correspondence, his art writings, the whimsical prose pieces collected in the *Moralités Légendaires*, as well as many of his quirky line-drawings. During his tragically foreshortened life, however, Laforgue managed to see just two volumes of his poetry into print, both at his own expense. The canny, but somewhat untrustworthy, Parisian publisher Léon Vanier issued *Les Complaintes* in July of 1885, some 18 months after the start of negotiations, and from the same firm came the much shorter *L'Imitation de Notre-Dame la Lune* around four months later (but with 1886 as the date of publication given on the title page). All but the last of his most original and influential sequence, the twelve *vers libre* poems grouped under the heading *Derniers Vers*, appeared piecemeal in the magazines *La Vogue* and the *Revue Indépendante* in the year before Laforgue died at the age of twenty-seven of tuberculosis (probably contracted from his English wife, Leah Lee). The significance of these final poems was only generally recognized, however, after Édouard Dujardin, one of Laforgue's staunchest admirers, put together the first posthumous editions of his work during the 1890s. A three-volume Mercure de France edition followed in 1901-03, and it was these tomes that the instantly smitten Eliot acquired from Paris in 1909, with spectacular results for modern poetry.

If Laforgue's destabilizing "art of the nerves" prefigures many aspects of the collage-style poetics developed and championed by Eliot and Pound in the early decades of the twentieth century, it also harks back to the work of Charles Baudelaire, another of the dominant French influences on Eliot's evolution. The impact of *Les Fleurs du Mal* is prominent in the early poems that Laforgue assembled into a posthumously published collection entitled *Le Sanglot de la Terre*, whose section headings, such as "Angoisses," "Poèmes de (Variations sur) la Mort," or "Spleen," obtrusively signal their origins in the jaundiced despair dramatized in Baudelaire's *Flowers of Evil*. I have included just one poem from this mass of juvenilia, the sonnet "La première nuit," which succinctly catches the young Laforgue's fusion of the cynical and the macabre: "*Voici venir le soir doux au vieillard lubrique* . . ." it opens, "Here comes evening, sweet to ageing lechers . . . ." The poem's final lines set up what would become a characteristically Laforguian oscillation: one moment he is thinking of all the babies who have just been born, the next he is imaginatively entering the coffins of newly buried corpses about to spend their first night underground.

It didn't, however, take Laforgue long to evolve far more nuanced and self-doubting versions of the dandy persona than the Baudelairean one that haunts the city streets of his adolescent imagination. The Pierrots who populate *Les Complaintes* and the later poems are prone to attacks of ennui or the spleen that are more often comic than corrosive, while the to-and-fro between Laforgue's lovers seesaws from exhilaration to irony, and only rarely strays into the realms of gothic excess that one finds in Baudelaire—or indeed in the Eliot of "Ode" or *The Waste Land*. Baudelaire was, nevertheless, to resurface in the last section of what turned out to be Laforgue's final poem, number XII of the *Derniers Vers*, which reangles a phrase from the concluding couplet of Baudelaire's "Un Voyage à Cythère"("*—Ah! Seigneur! donnez-moi la force et le courage / De contempler mon cœur et mon corps sans dégout!*") away from self-disgust towards what might be called self-reliance:

Ô Nature, donne-moi la force et le courage
De me croire en âge,
Ô Nature relève-moi le front!

I need, O Nature, strength
And courage to trust what the years
Have made of me . . . to look up, clear . . .

Such strength and courage are needed so that he can do justice to the life he hopes to share with his "*orpheline héroïne"*—like many of the *Derniers Vers*, the poem traces aspects of his burgeoning relationship with his English teacher, Leah Lee of Teignmouth, Devon, to whom he became engaged on 6 September 1886. Alas, despite this prayer, it was the poem's final line that was to prove prescient of their future together. Laforgue died just eight months after their wedding on New Year's Eve of that year, while Leah Lee outlived him by not quite ten months: "*Puisque, tôt ou tard, nous mourrons . . .*"

The kaleidoscopic narratives and quixotic oscillations in mood and tone that characterise Laforgue's lyrics undoubtedly refract his disjointed childhood. He was born in 1860 in Montevideo, Uruguay, the second son of the polyphiloprogenitive Charles and Pauline Laforgue—a further nine siblings would follow. In "Avertissement'," the opening poem of *Des Fleurs de Bonne Volonté,* Laforgue describes his father as *un dur par timidité,* a harsh man on account of his fearfulness, while of his mother he dryly observes that he barely knew her. Following the outbreak of war between Uruguay and Paraguay in 1866, it was decided that Charles, who worked in a bank, would remain in Montevideo while Pauline and the children (five at this stage) should return to Tarbes in the southwest of France, where Charles had family. After some two years and a few months this experiment in living apart was abandoned, but when Pauline boarded the slow boat back to Montevideo in 1869 it was without her two eldest sons: Émile and Jules were enrolled as boarders at the Tarbes lycée, where they remained for the next six years. Even school holidays offered little respite, for these were spent with Jules's least favourite relative, a baker called Pascal Darré. The family was not reunited until Charles and Pauline finally renounced their expatriate life in Uruguay once and for all, eventually settling in the Batignolles district of Paris in 1876. Pauline died the following year, at the age of thirty-nine, of pneumonia contracted after the miscarriage of what would have been her twelfth child, while Charles succumbed to angina pectoris five years later. "So now we're eleven orphans . . .," Laforgue wrote dolefully to his favourite sister, Marie, on being informed of his father's death.

It was during Laforgue's five years in Paris from 1876 to 1881 that he formed most of the artistic friendships that were to prove vital both to his literary development and to his poetic afterlife. Failure (twice) in his baccalaureate examinations meant that he was not able to attend university, instead joining his older brother Émile as a student at L'École des Beaux Arts. Both an ambitious autodidact and an early starter, by the age of twenty Laforgue had composed not only the hundreds of poems gathered in *Le Sanglot de la Terre* but a verse play entitled *Tessa*, as well as twenty-six *Chroniques Parisiennes* published in a magazine called *La Guêpe*. "My sole aim," he declared on his 1879 application for a reader's pass to the Bibliothèque Nationale, "is to become a writer."

His voracious reading during this period included, alongside Baudelaire, the philosophy of Schopenhauer and Eduard Von Hartmann, the poetry of Heine and Leconte de Lisle, and the fiction of J.-K Huysmans. By the end of the decade, he was regularly submitting articles, poems, and pen-drawings to journals, and attending literary gatherings such as that of the Hydropathes. His heady immersion in Parisian artistic life in turn led to friendships with the writers Gustave Kahn, Charles Henry, and Paul Bourget, who all bolstered his poetic ambitions and advised on work in progress. In the spring of 1881 Bourget introduced him to the wealthy connoisseur of the arts Charles Ephrussi (one of the models for Marcel Proust's Charles Swann) who offered Laforgue the role of part-time assistant. As well as an expert on Dürer and a contributor to the *Gazette des Beaux-Arts*, Ephrussi was an avid collector of Impressionist painters; adorning the walls of the elegant Hôtel Ephrussi at 81 rue de Monceau were works by such as Manet, Berthe Morisot, Monet, Renoir, Constantin Guys, Pissarro, Degas, Sisley, and Mary Cassatt. Laforgue may have lived during these months in a spartan garret in the Latin Quarter, but each morning he worked in a room hung with paintings by many of the most exciting artists of the era.

On the very day in mid-November of 1881 that Laforgue learned of his father's death he also received the improbable news that he had been appointed to be the next French Reader to the Empress Augusta at the Imperial Court of Prussia. This was courtesy of the manoeuvrings of Ephrussi and Bourget, and unfortunately meant, since he had to wait in Paris for instructions concerning travel arrangements to Germany, that he was unable to attend his father's funeral in Tarbes, to which the family had retreated when Laforgue senior fell ill. It must, then, have been with mixed feelings that he set off by train for Coblenz on 29 November 1881; there he was met by an antique palace coach and driven to a royal château, where a gold-braided footman led him to a stately suite of apartments in which a servant and his wife waited to greet him. It was a far, far cry from a room in a cheap hotel on rue Monsieur-le-Prince. The Reader's minimal daily duties, for which Laforgue received the princely sum of 9,000 francs a year, involved reading aloud from French newspapers, novels, biographies, and poems to the unashamedly Francophile Empress—although he also had to be careful that the passages he selected contained nothing scabrous or controversial. "I'm reading quite well," he recounted in a letter to Marie after his first audience with the Empress, "when oops! I see a risky bit just ahead . . . In masterly fashion, so that it isn't a bit obvious, I skip the risky bit. Saved! Oh my God!" His detailed letters back to Marie and to his friends in Paris suggest that, aside from his morning and evening sessions with the Empress, his time was pretty much his own. Initially this abrupt transition from an intellectually stimulating, if penurious and uncertain bohemian existence to one of splendid pomp and rigid etiquette seemed scarcely credible, and in a letter to Charles Henry written shortly after his arrival in Berlin, whither the Court moved on 1 December, he sounds almost like Alice in Wonderland:

> It's footmen, lights, great white staircases and mirrors, followed by mirrors, great white staircases, lights and footmen. I haven't had a moment's time for thought which is just as well, otherwise I might pass out in ecstasy.

Laforgue would remain in this peculiar post until September of 1886, following the Court in its annual peregrinations from Berlin, its main residence, to Baden Baden (which he hated) to Coblenz (which he adored) to Potsdam to Hamburg, and so on. As a salaried member of the Empress's entourage he travelled in style, lived always in spacious apartments (he notes that his high-ceilinged study in Coblenz was equipped with a "desk all ready for writing with a fine inkwell"), and wanted for nothing. Yet increasingly he came to feel frustrated by this pampered existence and the unreal routines that dominated his life. In comparison with Paris, Berlin seemed boring and provincial, and Laforgue wearied of the intrigues that dominated the Prussian Court. Germans, further, seemed immune to the delights of Impressionism, although his discovery in 1882 of the astonishing engraver Max Klinger, "genius of the bizarre," as he called him in a letter to Ephrussi, somewhat made up for this. The two became friends and exchanged letters. Klinger's sequence *The Glove* in many ways matches Laforgue's habit of sliding from scenes of social propriety into vignettes or tableaux that are hard to parse and verge on the surreal.

Over fifty poems in his first published volume are titled *complainte*, a term that dates back to medieval times and such as Guillaume de Machaut and Jean Froissart. Laforgue's lyrics in this mode are anything but archaic or backward-looking, combining the slang of the streets with dandyish conjugations of disaffection, or playing off eccentric lists such as those included in "Complainte de l'Automne monotone" with dreamy montages of subjectivity and uncertainty. It was in these poems that he first set about exploring the figure of the Pierrot, as in two of the poems selected here, "Complainte de Lord Pierrot" and "Autre Complainte de Lord Pierrot"—Laforgue was always delightfully unabashed about reusing titles, composing no fewer than sixteen poems called "Dimanches"! Lines and cadences of folksongs such as "Au clair de la lune" are also braided into the swaying, unpredictable progress of these extemporisations on regret and indecision. His dapper clown-dandies, even the aristocratic Lord Pierrot, tend to be comically adrift but consumed with yearning, and prone to extravagant fantasies of suddenly being sought out by some ideal woman determined on amorous possession:

Ah! qu'une, d'elle-même, un beau soir sût venir,
Ne voyant que boire à mes lèvres, ou mourir!

Ah, if only some fine evening just *one*
Of them would come to me, of her own
Free will, wishing to drink at my lips—or perish!

In best commedia dell'arte style, alas, such extravagant fancies ("I'd be (don't you agree?) the finest conquest / Ever made by woman") only end up occasioning a disappointment almost as extravagant: "My heart is as sad as a funfair / Paper lantern . . ." trails off "Complainte de Lord Pierrot," with the added twist that the poem ends with the instruction *(Bis)*, meaning the whole lament is to commence again at once.

It is not known to what extent the imagined or truncated or asymmetrical relationships traced in *Les Complaintes* relate to Laforgue's own amorous adventures in Germany. His Agenda (a kind of shorthand diary) of 1883 contains allusions to a woman referred to as R, with whom he enjoyed a "*grande scène*" on 27 May, and "*tendresses*'"on 30 and 31 May, and on 1 June too . . . She has been tentatively identified as Rosalie Maria Helena Bachem, one of the Empress's ladies-in-waiting, and the daughter of the Mayor of Coblenz—and twenty years older than Laforgue. Scholars have posited that it was R who is depicted waving goodbye to him with her pocket handkerchief at a parting between lovers on the Rhine in the third stanza of "Complainte d'un certain Dimanche," composed in July of that year. There are, at any rate, no more references to R in the Agenda after this date, and while mention is made of numerous other women in his Agenda and his correspondence, no further clues to the state of his affections emerge until he starts learning English with Leah Lee, and reports to his musician friend Eugène Ysaÿe, in January of 1886, that he is "*merveilleusement épris d'une jeune Anglaise.*"

L'Imitation de Notre-Dame la Lune was composed in a mere six weeks in the spring of 1885. This short volume intermingles Pierrot dialogues, like the brilliant "Pierrots" (subtitled "*Scène courte mais typique*") with the dizzying lunar speculations on display in such as "Clair de lune," which figures the moon as a dis-masted ship, as an ice-cold skull, as a pill promising ultimate rest to the agitated brain. Comic despair and a longing for some kind of reprieve from the burdens of self-consciousness and the dilemmas posed by love are dramatized in both sorts of poem; for, as Symons noted in *The Symbolist Movement in Literature*, the urge to escape in Laforgue often serves to express the painfulness of the quotidian:

> He has constructed his own world, lunar and actual, speaking slang and astronomy, with a constant disengaging of the visionary aspect, under which frivolity becomes an escape from the arrogance of a still more temporary mode of being, the world as it appears to the sober majority. He is terribly conscious of daily life, cannot omit, mentally, a single hour of the day; and his flight to the moon is in sheer desperation . . . And he sees, not only as an imposition, but a conquest, the possibilities for art which come from the sickly modern being, with his clothes, his nerves: the mere fact that he flowers from the soil of his epoch.

The "lunar and actual," in other words, cannot be disentangled, and it is from their interplay that Laforgue's ability to capture "sickly modern being" derives.

Although he had two volumes published in 1885, and received some glowing, as well as one or two sceptical reviews, along with congratulations from the highest priest of Symbolism, Stéphane Mallarmé, it was the following year that was truly Laforgue's *annus mirabilis.* Perhaps under the influence of the English Leah Lee, Laforgue's lunar Pierrot now found its most rewarding prototype in Shakespeare's Hamlet, and carefully chosen quotations from this play cast, via epigraphs, their inky cloak over the poems that he collected in both *Des Fleurs de Bonne Volonté* (its title a tongue-in-cheek reversal of Baudelaire's flowers of evil) and his *Derniers Vers,* which is prefaced by Ophelia's account of the melancholy prince's taking of her wrist, lengthy perusal of her face, and sigh "so piteous and profound, / That it did seem to shatter all his bulk, / And end his being." A poem such as the ironically titled "Romance," whose epigraph is Hamlet's cruel injunction to Ophelia, "To a nunnery, go," offers a disturbing example of what Eliot would call the "sordid images" that confound attempts to reduce the male sexual imagination to the comforting tropes of bourgeois romantic literature. Laforgue's unnerving description of his soul populated by nesting or circling seabirds and foul with stinking carrion can be read as an oblique gloss on the sexual problems bedevilling Shakespeare's hero, while also looking forward to a poem such as Philip Larkin's "If, My Darling," in which the speaker frankly describes his sexual consciousness as opaque and unwholesome, "looped with the creep of varying light, / Monkey-brown, fish-grey, a string of infected circles . . . ." Larkin, despite his much-vaunted dislike of foreign literature, once characterized himself as "the Laforgue of Pearson Park" (the district where he lived in Hull), and, in their willingness to revolve aspects of the male psyche in a manner at once radical and disturbing, Laforgue's *Hamlet*-inspired poems prefigure the bracing honesty of some of the early Larkin's depictions of masculine erotic confusion as well as his later indulgence in unregulated flights of sexual fancy.

Laforgue's *Derniers Vers* make use of a number of the lines and images deployed in *Des Fleurs de Bonne Volonté*, which he didn't attempt to publish. Although linked by these echoes and self-borrowings, and both composed in 1886, there is a vast difference between the earlier and the later sequence, for it was in the *Derniers Vers* that Laforgue first started using free verse or *vers libre*: "I forget to rhyme," he wrote to Gustave Kahn in August of that year, "I forget the number of syllables, I forget to set it in stanzas—the lines themselves begin in the margin just like prose . . . I'm working on nothing else . . . And I'll never write poetry any different from what I'm writing now." Crucial to this development was his immersion in the poetry of Walt Whitman; that summer Kahn's magazine, *La Vogue*, published, in three instalments, Laforgue's translations of ten Whitman poems, including the controversial "A Woman Waits for Me," which had led to the censorship of Whitman's work in America. These versions from *Les Brins d'Herbes*, as he called *Leaves of Grass*, are prefaced in *La Vogue* by the admiring note, "*Traduit de l'étonnant poète américain Walt Whitman*." And a further catalyst for this startling breakthrough was surely Arthur Rimbaud's *Illuminations*, which were also published in various issues of *La Vogue* that year. "*Comme il est entier!*," Laforgue marvelled of the enfant terrible, "*presque sans rhétorique et sans attaches*."

Laforgue himself was about to enter into an *attache* or tie that would transform his life. After much Prufrockian dithering, and shared outings to the opera and concerts and museums of Berlin, he and his English teacher came to an understanding that meant he had to renounce his post as Reader to the Empress, the holder of which could not be married. The exhilarating collages of the *Derniers Vers* reflect Laforgue's excitement at the *vita nuova* on which he was considering embarking (they date mainly from his courtship of Leah Lee), and their repeated use of hunting cries such as *Taïaut!* and *Hallali!* or what sound like nonsense formulations ("*Armorial d'anémie!*" or "*Emballages, dévergondages, douches!*") viscerally express the urge to move beyond the imprisoning modes of self-consciousness so fully dramatized in his earlier work, rather as Wallace Stevens used phrases such as "hoo-hoo-hoo" or "shoo-shoo-shoo" or "ric-a-nic" or "ding, ding, dong" to intimate aurally worlds or experiences beyond reason. I have included here versions of all twelve of the *Derniers Vers*. Laforgue was himself aware that in these poems he was at his most daring, inventive, and original, and that the free-flowing idiom and intricate rhythmic patterns they develop were a new step in the evolution of French poetry. The responses of his literary friends confirmed this, and their admiration emboldened him in his decision to set up as *un homme de lettres* in Paris.

My favourite is probably "Solo de lune," a title I have translated as "Lunar Solo." It traces a coach journey between unnamed destinations, in the course of which the speaker broods on various contretemps and misunderstandings in his wooing of a girl who is suffering from a persistent cough. These swirling self-recriminations and regrets are like subtitles or a voice-over as the landscape streams by, captured in electrically charged but seemingly haphazard rhymes, as if the poet's nerves, to borrow Symons's term, and what he witnesses were fused into a single flowing process:

La lune se lève,
Ô route en grand rêve!
Ô route sans terme,
Voici le relais,
Où l'on allume les lanternes,
Où l'on boit un verre de lait,
Et fouette postillon,
Dans le chant des grillons,
Sous les étoiles de Juillet.

The moon rises
Above the oneiric, endless
Road—we reach
A staging post, and lighted
Lanterns, a glass of milk, and cries
Of 'Drive, postilion,
Drive!' amid chirping
Crickets, beneath the stars
Of July.

The feel of being not only *in medias res* but in jolting, rapid motion that the poem communicates is as astoundingly vivid as anything in Whitman. In this poem Laforgue twice compares his dancing soul to that of Ariel (so clearly he'd read *The Tempest* as well as *Hamlet*) and there is "*de la magie*" indeed in its mercurial shifts of register and scene, the way it cuts between journey and reminiscence, between rapturous addresses to the moon and speculations about the doings of his beloved. If she's walking alone in a forest at night,

Elle aura oublié son foulard,
Elle va prendre mal, vu la beauté de l'heure!
Oh! soigne-toi je t'en conjure!
Oh! Je ne veux plus entendre cette toux!

. . . she'll have forgotten
Her scarf and the night's beauties
Will have her rapt in wonder . . . she'll catch cold, oh please
Take care—what I would give never again to have to hear
Your coughing.

Stray references to Leah Lee's *petite toux sèche maligne*—her little, malign, dry cough—occasionally sound a note of alarm and foreboding in these richly symphonic poems, through which Laforgue seems both to be charting the vacillations of their courtship and wondering only semi-ironically how to transform himself into "*le modèle des epoux*," the paragon of husbands.

Leah Lee returned to England on 2 October. It had been agreed that they would marry in London, in St Barnabas Church in Kensington (where, by coincidence, T.S. Eliot was to wed his second wife Valerie just over seventy years later), on the last day of the year. In a letter to his sister Marie written two days after he had proposed and been accepted, Laforgue declared that his fiancée is "*un petit personnage impossible à décrire*," but then goes on to itemize her chestnut hair with red tints in it, her slender neck, her mischievous smile, her big eyes (the colour of tar), her distinguished manners, her shyness, her thinness, her attractive candour (although it later emerged that she was three years older than the age of twenty-two that she put down on their marriage certificate), her quiet voice, and her funny little accent when she spoke French. He also explained the urgency of her leaving Berlin: "*Elle tousse un peu et ne doit pas passer un autre hiver ici.*" After seeing her onto the boat at Calais, Laforgue returned to Paris, where he arranged lodgings for his prospective bride at 8 rue de Commaille in the 7th arrondissement. Despite the handsome salary that he'd received during his five years as Reader to the Empress, Laforgue's savings seem to have been non-existent, and the months before setting off for London were spent desperately trying to secure employment and fee-paying writing commissions, with disappointing results. Leah herself had not a *sou* to her name, having abandoned her family in disgust after her father (a well-to-do draper from Teignmouth) had rather too precipitately—to her mind at least—married the children's governess following the death of her mother in 1883. Laforgue was driven to apply to his family for a loan, which was eventually granted. More concerning still, he himself was suffering from a cough and a cold which refused to clear up.

Laforgue arrived early on the morning of his wedding in a snowy, foggy, bitterly cold London. His Anglophilia had little time to be corrected by the realities of life in England, for the newly married couple caught the 6:30 evening boat train from Charing Cross on 2 January, reaching Paris the next morning, bedraggled and ill. If 1886 saw the flowering of his gifts as a writer, as well as the burgeoning of his love and the overcoming of his habits of procrastination and indecisiveness, 1887 was catastrophic in every way. His health deteriorated rapidly, and he was forced to send out what were effectively begging letters to such as Ephrussi, Bourget, and Édouard Dujardin. He even dispatched, the day before he died, a plea to the Minister for Public Instruction for a grant from a fund established for men of letters in distress. A leading tuberculosis specialist, Dr Albert Robin, agreed to treat the impecunious poet for free, but all that could be prescribed were opium pills, which left him feeling drained of energy. While the illusion that after spending the winter in North Africa he would be on the road to recovery was nobly maintained by friends and family, as well as by his "gay and whimsical" wife, the end was in fact fast approaching. His older brother Émile shared with Leah sickbed duties, and left a heart-wrenching record of Laforgue's weakening state:

> Up until the last day my brother thought he would get over his illness. He refused to go to bed, preferring to spend his days in a chair, in the desperate hope that he could do some work. He also made plans to go to Algiers, and even fixed a date for the departure.
>
> One morning, the day before his death, I arrived at the flat and surprised him in the act of trying on his wedding ring, which had become too big for his wasted fingers and which he had removed long before.

After firing off his final request for money to the Minister for Public Instruction on 19 August, a clearly bewildered Laforgue remarked: "I am not seeing things as I used to. I am not thinking the same way, either. Oh, you'll see . . . You will see the things I shall write now!" His final utterance, around six o'clock on the following morning, was, "I think I'm hallucinating . . ." "Five minutes later," Émile records, "it was all over."

In December of that year, Leah contacted Teodor de Wyzewa, a literary friend of Laforgue's. She herself was heading to Menton in the South of France in a futile quest for better health, and before leaving Paris wanted to deposit with Wyzewa, who was one of the founder-editors of the *Revue Indépendante* in which two of her husband's *Derniers Vers* had appeared, his surviving manuscripts. Wyzewa duly visited her in the Hôtel de Londres et Milan where she was staying, and the case of papers was handed over. By the spring of 1888, her *petite toux sèche* had become seriously *maligne*. She returned in April to London, where she entered St Paul's Convent in Kilburn, and there she died on 6 June. The following week she was buried beside her mother in her native Teignmouth.

Acknowledgements and a Note on These Versions

Much of the information above derives from David Arkell's *Looking for Laforgue* (1979). It was Arkell who cleared up a number of the mysteries surrounding Leah Lee, and who discovered her burial place in Teignmouth Old Cemetery in the grave plots purchased by her father Samuel Lee in 1883. All anglophone admirers of Laforgue owe a great debt to Arkell for his pioneering research and for his lucid account of the French poet's life and work.

I would like also to acknowledge the advice and assistance of Neil Rennie, Alan Jenkins, and of Suzannah V. Evans, whose suggestions greatly improved my versions of the twenty-five poems included here. Three of these ("Complainte-Litanies de mon Sacré-Cœur," "Avant-dernier mot," and *Derniers Vers* IX [Oh! qu'une, d'Elle-même . . .]) appeared in *All Keyboards Are Legitimate: Versions of Jules Laforgue* edited by Suzannah V. Evans and published by Guillemot Press, UK (2023). This excellent volume contains translations by such as Christopher Reid, Hannah Sullivan, Vidyan Ravinthiran, and Douglas Dunn, and an Afterword by Clive Scott that discusses the problems presented to translators by the 'polyphonic or heteroglossic' aspects of Laforgue's idiom.

I am grateful to Suzannah for re-igniting my long-dormant interest in Laforgue; the pleasure I derived from translating the three poems I was allocated prompted this attempt to create versions of a more substantial selection. I also learned a great deal about T.S. Eliot's responses to Laforgue from Suzannah's PhD thesis, *T.S. Eliot and the Implications of Laforgue and Corbière* (2022).

In 2011 I published a parallel text edition of Raymond Roussel's final long poem, *Nouvelles Impressions d'Afrique* (Princeton University Press). In translating that work, which is in rhyming hexameters but makes disorientating use of numerous brackets and wildly digressive footnotes, themselves rhymed, my primary intention was to convey the meaning of each of the many examples that make up the substance of Roussel's four cantos. Such a poem offers no scope for creative interpretation. I have adopted a somewhat different approach for this parallel text edition of Jules Laforgue. My overriding concern was to create versions that register as effective poems. Readers can tell what liberties I have taken by glancing across from the English on the recto to the French on the verso—and then judge whether they believe these liberties warranted. Anyone seeking more rigorously literal translations should seek out Graham Dunstan Martin's 1998 edition for Penguin Books, which presents a prose version beneath each of the poems selected.

I cannot help hoping that this book will inspire in those unfamiliar with Laforgue's œuvre, or who know him only through his influence on Eliot's apprentice work and first published poems, a response somewhat akin to J-K. Huysmans's exclamation: "*Jules Laforgue—Quelle joie!*"

from

Le Sanglot de la Terre /
The Sob of the Earth (1880)

La première nuit

Sonnet

Voici venir le soir doux au vieillard lubrique.
Mon chat Mürr, accroupi comme un sphinx héraldique,
Contemple inquiet de sa prunelle fantastique
Monter à l'horizon la lune chlorotique.

C'est l'heure où l'enfant prie, où Paris-Lupanar
Jette sur le pavé de chaque boulevard
Les filles aux seins froids qui sous le gaz blafard
Vaguent flairant de l'œil un mâle de hasard.

Moi, près de mon chat Mürr, je rêve à ma fenêtre.
Je songe aux enfants qui partout viennent de naître,
Je songe à tous les morts enterrés d'aujourd'hui.

Et je me figure être au fond du cimetière
Et me mets à la place en entrant dans leur bière
De ceux qui vont passer là leur première nuit.

The First Night

Sonnet

Here comes evening, sweet to ageing lechers.
My cat Mürr, crouched like a heraldic
Sphinx, seems nervous, his fantastical pupils rapt
By the chlorotic moon ascending on the horizon.

It is the hour when children pray, the hour when icy-
Breasted girls issue from Parisian bordellos
Onto the murky, gas-lit boulevards
In quest of a drifting male.

Mürr at my side, I dream at my window.
I think of all those newly born, and of all
The dead who were buried today.

I picture myself deep in the graveyard,
And I see myself entering, at will, the coffins
Of those spending their first night underground.

from

Les Complaintes / *The Laments* (1885)

Complainte d'un certain Dimanche

'Elle ne concevait pas qu'aimer fût l'ennemi d'aimer.'

SAINTE-BEUVE, *VOLUPTÉ*

L'homme n'est pas méchant, ni la femme éphémère.
Ah! fous dont au casino battent les talons,
Tout homme pleure un jour et toute femme est mère,
Nous sommes tous filials, allons!
Mais quoi! Les Destins ont des partis-pris si tristes,
Qui font que, les uns loin des autres, l'on s'exile,
Qu'on se traite à tort et à travers d'égoïstes,
Et qu'on s'use à trouver quelque unique Évangile.
Ah! jusqu'à ce que la nature soit bien bonne,
Moi je veux vivre monotone.

Dans ce village en falaises, loin, vers les cloches,
Je redescends dévisagé par les enfants
Qui s'en vont faire bénir de tièdes brioches;
Et rentré, mon sacré-cœur se fend!
Les moineaux des vieux toits pépient à ma fenêtre,
Ils me regardent dîner, sans faim, à la carte;
Des âmes d'amis morts les habitent peut-être?
Je leur jette du pain: comme blessés, ils partent!
Ah! jusqu'à ce que la nature soit bien bonne,
Moi je veux vivre monotone.

Lament of a Certain Sunday

"She didn't realize that to love was the enemy of loving."

SAINTE-BEUVE, *VOLUPTÉ*

Man is not evil, nor woman
Ephemeral. You fools drumming your heels
In casinos – all men cry one day, and every woman
Finds herself *mother*: we are all
        Somebody's children.
What of it – except alas? Our ends
Are predetermined, meaning
We drift apart, into exile, malign
Each other's egotism, grow weary
Of searching for some unique, infallible gospel. *Until Nature*
Behaves kindly, dull dull dull
        My life will be.

I'm in a distant cliff-top village, and making
My way down towards the clanging bells, and being
Gawped at by children wanting
Their warm brioches blessed.
        Home, and my *sacred heart* breaks.
Sparrows twitter on the ancient roofs outside
My window, and watch me dine, without hunger, off
Whatever. Could it be they harbour
The souls of dead friends? When I throw them bread
They scatter, as if offended. *Until Nature*
Behaves kindly, dull dull dull
        My life will be.

Elle est partie hier. Suis-je pas triste d'elle?
Mais c'est vrai! Voilà donc le fond de mon chagrin!
Oh! ma vie est aux plis de ta jupe fidèle!
Son mouchoir me flottait sur le Rhin . . .
Seul. – Le Couchant retient un moment son Quadrige
En rayons où le ballet des moucherons danse,
Puis, vers les toits fumants de la soupe, il s'afflige . . .
Et c'est le Soir, l'insaisissable confidence . . .
Ah! jusqu'à ce que la nature soit bien bonne,
Faudra-t-il vivre monotone?

Que d'yeux, en éventail, en ogive, ou d'inceste,
Depuis que l'Être espère, ont réclamé leurs droits!
Ô ciels, les yeux pourrissent-ils comme le reste?
Oh! qu'il fait seul! Oh! fait-il froid!
Oh! que d'après-midi d'automne à vivre encore!
Le Spleen, eunuque à froid, sur nos rêves se vautre!
Or, ne pouvant redevenir des madrépores,
Ô mes humains, consolons-nous les uns les autres.
Et jusqu'à ce que la nature soit bien bonne,
Tâchons de vivre monotone.

She left yesterday. How sad should – how sad *does*
That make me? Can I sound the depths
Of my hurt? . . . my life is forever bound up
In the pleats of her skirt . . . from the Rhine
            She waved at me her pocket handkerchief . . .
Alone, I watch the setting sun restrain
A moment its chariot – while midges pirouette
In its dying rays – then swoon, grieving,
Towards housetops swathed
In soupy fumes. Aha, elusive, secretive evening is here . . . *Until Nature*
Behaves kindly, must
            My life be dull dull dull?

From behind fans, beneath a lancet arch, inflamed
With incest, eyes, since hope
Was born, have demanded
Rights. And do eyes putrify, like the rest of us?
            It's lonesome, here, and cold . . .
Autumn afternoons . . . how many remain
To be lived through? That frosty eunuch, spleen,
Sprawls on our dreams. If we cannot go back, become
Polyps in some reef – let us, O humanity, at the very least
Console each other . . . *And until Nature*
Behaves kindly, let's try
            To be dull dull dull.

Complainte de l'Automne monotone

Automne, automne, adieux de l'Adieu!
La tisane bout, noyant mon feu;
        Le vent s'époumonne
A reverdir la bûche où mon grand cœur tisonne.
        Est-il de vrais yeux?
Nulle ne songe à m'aimer un peu.

        Milieux aptères,
        Ou sans divans;
        Regards levants,
        Deuils solitaires,
        Vers des Sectaires!

Le vent, la pluie, oh! le vent, la pluie!
Antigone, écartez mon rideau;
        Cet ex-ciel tout suie,
Fond-il *decrescendo, statu quo, crescendo?*
        Le vent qui s'ennuie,
Retourne-t-il bien les parapluies?

Lament of the Dreary Autumn

Autumn, autumn – saying goodbye
To "goodbye" itself. The tea boils over, dousing
My fire, and the wind
        Yells itself hoarse, as if urging
The log stirred into flames by my sorrowing heart
To sprout leaves again. Can eyes
        Be true – be real? . . . there's no one
Thinks of loving me, at all, at all . . .

        Wingless
        Places – lacking
        Divans – dawning
        Glances – deaths endured
        Alone – verses
        Of the sectarian kind . . .

Wind, rain . . . more wind, more rain, aaagh!
Antigone, draw back my curtain . . . a sky
That *was*, as black
        As soot,
Melting – falling – rising – staying
The same . . . when the wind
        Grows bored, will it keep
Turning umbrellas inside out?

Amours, gibiers!
Aux jours de givre,
Rêver sans livre,
Dans les terriers
Chauds de fumiers!

Plages, chemins de fer, ciels, bois morts,
Bateaux croupis dans les feuilles d'or,
Le quart aux étoiles,
Paris grasseyant par chic aux prises de voiles:
De trop poignants cors
M'ont hallalisé ces chers décors.

Meurtres, alertes,
Rêves ingrats!
En croix, les bras;
Roses ouvertes,
Divines pertes!

Loves – prey – frosty
Days – dreaming
Bookless – ensconced
In steaming
Burrows tunnelled
Into dunghills . . .

Dead wood, beaches, skies,
Railways, boats mouldering
In golden, autumn leaves . . . night
Watches amid the stars . . .
Paris, fashionable Paris rolling its rs at the taking
Of veils . . . *Hallali* – I hear
The too poignant horns
Trumpet the demise of these cherished facades . . .

Murders – alerts –
Ungrateful
Dreams – crossed
Arms and open
Roses – losses –
That are divine . . .

Le soleil mort, tout nous abandonne.
Il se crut incompris. Qu'il est loin!
        Vent pauvre, aiguillonne
Ces convois de martyrs se prenant à témoins!
        La terre, si bonne,
S'en va, pour sûr, passer cet automne.

        Nuits sous-marines!
        Pourpres forêts,
        Torrents de frais,
        Bancs en gésines,
        Tout s'illumine!

– Allons, fumons une pipette de tabac,
En feuilletant un de ces si vieux almanachs,

En rêvant de la petite qui unirait
Aux charmes de l'œillet ceux du chardonneret.

The sun being dead, we
Are left alone. *He* considered himself
Misunderstood. How very far away he is now . . .
        Meagre wind, keep on
Goading processions of martyrs to deliver their
Accounts of each other . . . but this
        Good earth
For certain, is nearing its end this autumn.

        Submarine
        Nights – forests
        Deep maroon –
        A torrent
        Of costs – shoals
        Unfolding – all
        Is lit up . . .

Come – come – together let us smoke our pipes
While leafing through these old almanacs, dreaming

Of a dreamy girl . . . one who combines
The charms of a goldfinch with those
Of a marigold.

Complainte de Lord Pierrot

Au clair de la lune,
Mon ami Pierrot,
Filons, en costume,
Présider là-haut!
Ma cervelle est morte.
Que le Christ l'emporte!
Béons à la Lune,
La bouche en zéro.

Inconscient, descendez en nous par reflexes;
Brouillez les cartes, les dictionnaires, les sexes.

Tournons d'abord sur nous-même, comme un fakir!
(Agiter le pauvre être, avant de s'en servir.)

J'ai le cœur chaste et vrai comme une bonne lampe;
Oui, je suis en taille-douce, comme une estampe.

Vénus, énorme comme le Régent,
Déjà se pâme à l'horizon des grèves;
Et c'est l'heure, ô gens nés casés, bonnes gens,
De s'étourdir en longs trilles de rêves!
Corybanthe, aux quatre vents tous les draps!
Disloque tes pudeurs, à bas les lignes!

Lament of Lord Pierrot

By the light of the moon
My friend Pierrot, let us go
In costume and preside on doings
Up above. My brain
Is kaput – would to Christ
He would take it away! Meanwhile, round-
Mouthed, open-
Mouthed let's gape at the moon.

Unconscious – descend and enter
Via our reflexes, scramble the cards, the lexicons, even
The sexes.

But first, dervish-like, let's whirl around
And around – give the poor being a shake
Before serving.

My heart is as chaste and trustworthy as a good lamp . . . yes
Siree, I'm a print engraved
In copperplate.

Venus, like an enormous diamond, is already
A-swoon where the shoreline
Meets the sky. It's time for you decent, long-
Confined folk to be ravished by dulcet, soaring
Dreams, to dance like Corybants – open
Your sails to the wind! Down with this line

En costume blanc, je ferai le cygne,
Après nous le Déluge, ô ma Léda!
Jusqu'à ce que tournent tes yeux vitreux,
Que tu grelottes en rires affreux,
Hop! Enlevons sur les horizons fades
Les menuets de nos pantalonades!
Tiens! L'univers
Est à l'envers . . .

– Tout cela vous honore,
Lord Pierrot, mais encore?

– Ah! qu'une, d'elle-même, un beau soir sût venir,
Ne voyant que boire à mes lèvres, ou mourir!

Je serais, savez-vous, la plus noble conquête
Que femme, au plus ravi du Rêve, eût jamais faite!

D'ici-là, qu'il me soit permis
De vivre de vieux compromis.

Où commence, où finit l'humaine
Ou la divine dignité?

Jonglons avec les entités,
Pierrot s'agite et Tout le mène!
Laissez faire, laissez passer;

Or that! – dismantle your modesties! I'll
Dress up in an all-white swan costume, O
My Leda! – *Après nous le Déluge.* Until
Your eyes turn glassy, and you shiver
With dreadful laughter, *up up up* – let the bleak
Horizons resound to our fast and furious pantomime!
Tiens! The world
Turned upside down!

"All this honours you, my Lord
Pierrot – but then what?"

Ah, if only some fine evening just *one*
Of them would come to me, of her own
Free will, wishing to drink at my lips – or perish!

I'd be (don't you agree?) the finest conquest
Ever made by woman – would exceed
Her wildest erotic fantasy!

Until then, however, my humble
Wish is to bumble
Along in the standard compromised way.

Human dignity, divine dignity, where
Does either begin or end?

As you see, we
Can play at juggling entities . . . In thrall to all, Pierrot
Is clearly ill at ease. Let be, let be – for

Laissez passer, et laissez faire;
Le semblable, c'est le contraire,

Et l'univers, c'est pas assez!
Et je me sens, ayant pour cible
Adopté la vie impossible,
De moins en moins localisé!

– Tout cela vous honore,
Lord Pierrot, mais encore?

– Il faisait, ah! si chaud, si sec.
Voici qu' il pleut, qu'il pleut, bergères!
Les pauvres Vénus bocagères
Ont la roupie à leur nez grec!

– Oh! De moins en moins drôle;
Pierrot sait mal son rôle?

– J'ai le cœur triste comme un lampion forain . . .
Bah! J'irai passer la nuit dans le premier train;

Sûr d'aller, ma vie entière,
Malheureux comme les pierres. (*Bis.*)

Whatever *is* is both
Similar *and* the contrary . . .

This universe is, well, not
Enough. I'm feeling – my goal being the life
Impossible – less and less concerned
With the local.

"All this honours you, my Lord
Pierrot – but then what?"

It was so hot, so dry, but now
Il pleut, il pleut, bergères . . . and poor
Rural Venuses, your
Aquiline noses are dripping, dripping . . .

"Oh Pierrot, this is becoming less and less droll –
Have you forgotten your lines, your role?"

My heart is as sad as a funfair
Paper lantern . . . Bah! I'll spend
The night in the first train I find; and I

Can guarantee
That unhappy
I will be – my whole
Life long – as despondent
As a stone. (*Repeat*)

Autre Complainte de Lord Pierrot

Celle qui doit me mettre au courant de la Femme!
Nous lui dirons d'abord, de mon air le moins froid:
«La somme des angles d'un triangle, chère âme,
«Est égale à deux droits.»

Et si ce cri lui part: «Dieu de Dieu! que je t'aime!»
– «Dieu reconnaîtra les siens.» Ou piquée au vif:
– «Mes claviers ont du cœur, tu seras mon seul thème.»
Moi: «Tout est relatif.»

De tous ses yeux, alors! se sentant trop banale:
«Ah! tu ne m'aimes pas; tant d'autres sont jaloux!»
Et moi, d'un œil qui vers l'Inconscient s'emballe:
«Merci, pas mal; et vous?»

– «Jouons au plus fidèle!» – «A quoi bon, ô Nature!
«Autant à qui perd gagne!» Alors, autre couplet:
– «Ah! tu te lasseras le premier, j'en suis sûre . . .»
- «Après vous, s'il vous plaît.»

Enfin, si, par un soir, elle meurt dans mes livres,
Douce; feignant de n'en pas croire encor mes yeux,
J'aurai un: «Ah ça, mais, nous avions De Quoi vivre!
«C'était donc sérieux?»

Another Lament of Lord Pierrot

To her who will keep me au fait
With what concerns "the woman of today," I plan
In my least frigid tones, to say:
"In a triangle the sum of the angles, dear
　　　　Soul, equals two right angles."

And if she comes to me exclaiming, "God oh *God*
How I love you!," then "*Bien*, the Lord knows his own." Or,
Touched to the very core, "My *keyboard*
Is my beating heart, and *you* my inspiration!"
　　　　From me: "All is relative . . ."

Then, scrutinizing me, feeling she's sliding
Into cliché: "You *don't* love me – so many others, and all this
Jealousy . . ." At which I fix
An implacable eye on the UNCONSCIOUS and reply:
　　　　"Not at all bad, thank you, yes, and you?"

"Let's banter – about, say, fidelity?" "O Nature –
What would be the use?" "How about 'Loser
Ends Up Winning,' then?" Another
Couplet follows: "You'll get bored of me first, I'm sure!"
　　　　"No no, not at all, after you, my dear!"

And finally, if one night, peacefully, amidst my books, she were
To die . . . Feigning I could not credit
What I saw, I'd whisper: "Surely, surely
We had the means to live!
　　　　Was it *so* very serious?"

Complainte-Litanies de mon Sacré-Cœur

Prométhée et Vautour, châtiment et blasphème,
Mon Cœur, cancer sans cœur, se grignote lui-même.

Mon Cœur est une urne où j'ai mis certains défunts,
Oh! chut, refrains de leurs berceaux! et vous, parfums . . .

Mon Cœur est un lexique où cent littératures
Se lardent sans répit de divines ratures.

Mon Cœur est un désert altéré, bien que soûl
De ce vin revomi, l'universel dégoût.

Mon Cœur est un Néron, enfant gâté d'Asie,
Qui d'empires de rêve en vain se rassasie.

Mon Cœur est un noyé vidé d'âme et d'essors,
Qu'étreint la pieuvre Spleen en ses ventouses d'or.

C'est un feu d'artifice, hélas! qu'avant la fête,
A noyé sans retour l'averse qui s'embête.

Mon Cœur est le terrestre Histoire-Corbillard,
Que traînent au néant l'instinct et le hasard.

Mon Cœur est une horloge oubliée à demeure,
Qui, me sachant défunt, s'obstine à sonner l'heure!

My Sacred Heart: A Lament-Litany

Both Prometheus the blasphemer *and* the vulture at his liver,
My heart is a pitiless cancer, nibbling itself away.

It's a casket in which I've buried the once-living: *Hush oh hush*,
I whisper, at the sound of cradlesong, at the memory of scent.

Or else it's like some voracious literary algorithm, at work
On the entire canon: *delete – delete – delete –*

A thirsty wasteland gulping winy vomit, drunk
On disgust.

Now it's Nero, or some childish Eastern potentate,
Stuffing itself with endless, pointless dreams;

Now a drowned corpse, drifting, on which the octopus
(Spleen) is fastening its glistening suckers;

Now, literally, a damp squib! – an unused firework
Left out in the pummelling rain.

And if history is a hearse, so is my heart, dragged
This way and that, by instinct, by chance.

It's an unwound, forgotten clock, that knows
I'm defunct – but keeps on striking the hours.

Mon aimée était là, toute à me consoler;
Je l'ai trop fait souffrir, ça ne peut plus aller.

Mon Cœur, plongé au Styx de nos arts danaïdes,
Présente à tout baiser une armure de vide.

Et toujours, mon Cœur, ayant ainsi déclamé,
En revient à sa complainte: Aimer, être aimé!

Yet how deeply she suffered, my sweetheart (this cannot
Go on) when she sweetly came to console me;

For then my heart was a void, a hollow suit of armour
To her kiss, the blank waters of the Styx, running away . . .

And now, of course – this proclamation done – my heart returns
To its lament: to love . . . to be loved . . .

from

L'Imitation de Notre-Dame la Lune / The Imitation of Our Lady the Moon (1886)

Clair de lune

Penser qu'on vivra jamais dans cet astre,
Parfois me flanque un coup dans l'épigastre.

Ah! tout pour toi, Lune, quand tu t'avances
Aux soirs d'août par les féeries du silence!

Et quand tu roules, démâtée, au large
A travers les brisants noirs des nuages!

Oh! monter, perdu, m'étancher à même
Ta vasque de béatifiants baptêmes!

Astre atteint de cécité, fatal phare
Des vols migrateurs des plaintifs Icare!

Œil stérile comme le suicide,
Nous sommes le congrès des las, préside;

Crâne glacé, raille les calvities
De nos incurables bureaucraties;

Ô pilule des léthargies finales,
Infuse-toi dans nos durs encéphales!

Ô Diane à la chlamyde très-dorique,
L'Amour cuve, prend ton carquois et pique

Moonlight

Will we ever live on that star? – the thought
Itself has me reeling.

But Moon, when you move through August's
Evening skies in enchanting silence, I salute you!

Also when you career, like some dismasted ship,
Through heaving black breakers of cloud!

Oh to ascend, one of the lost, and slake
My thirst on your baptismal moonshine!

Stricken by blindness, your beacon is lethal
To Icarus-types, left stranded and grieving.

Sterile suicide-eye – preside
Over convocations of the world-weary.

Ice-cold skull, heap ridicule on our bald
And terminally ill bureaucracies.

O pill of ultimate fatigue, infuse
Yourself into our stubborn brains.

And chlamys-clad Diana, fermenting
Love unleashes barbs from your quiver

Ah! d'un trait inoculant l'être aptère,
Les cœurs de bonne volonté sur terre!

Astre lavé par d'inouïs déluges,
Qu'un de tes chastes rayons fébrifuges,

Ce soir, pour inonder mes draps, dévie,
Que je m'y lave les mains de la vie!

Which infect – ah! – the wingless, the hearts of those
Who would do good on earth!

Star prone to unheard of floods, I pray
That one of your chaste, anti-febrile rays veers, tonight,

In my direction, drenches my sheets, drives
Me to wash my hands of life!

Pierrots

(Scène courte, mais typique)

Il me faut vos yeux! Dès que je perds leur étoile,
Le mal des calmes plats s'engouffre dans ma voile,
Le frisson du *Væ soli!* gargouille en mes moelles . . .

Vous auriez dû me voir après cette querelle!
J'errais dans l'agitation la plus cruelle,
Criant aux murs: Mon Dieu! mon Dieu! Que dira-t-elle?

Mais aussi, vrai, vous me blessâtes aux antennes
De l'âme, avec les mensonges de votre traîne,
Et votre tas de complications mondaines.

Je voyais que vos yeux me lançaient sur des pistes,
Je songeais: oui, divins, ces yeux! mais rien n'existe
Derrière! Son âme est affaire d'oculiste.

Moi, je suis laminé d'esthétiques loyales!
Je hais les trémolos, les phrases nationales;
Bref, le violet gros deuil est ma couleur locale.

Je ne suis point «ce gaillard-là!» ni Le Superbe!
Mais mon âme, qu'un cri un peu cru exacerbe,
Est au fond distinguée et franche comme une herbe.

Pierrots

(A short but typical scene)

How I need your eyes! Losing them is like losing
A star – it leaves me flat, ill, becalmed, my sails windless,
While "woe to the lonely" rumbles in my marrow-bones.

If only you'd seen me after our tiff! I wandered
Around, distracted, in pain, moaning
To the walls, "Lord oh Lord, what *ever* will she say?"

But then my soul's antennae *had* been wounded
By you, and by the lies that shadow your every move – plus
Dealing with all your social "complications, complexities" and so on.

Further, it struck me your eyes were sending me down
All kinds of rabbit-hole: "Divine these eyes may be," I mused, "but only
An oculist could see the soul behind them – if it exists at all!"

In contrast, *my* sound artistic credos are laminated
All over me: I dislike the use of tremolo and all patriotic guff;
Deep purple mourning, in short, is my standard look.

I'm neither a roustabout nor some Übermensch; yet
My soul, which a slightly harsh cry can unsettle, is,
Basically, both noble and as candid as a blade of grass.

J'ai des nerfs encor sensibles au son des cloches,
Et je vais en plein air sans peur et sans reproche,
Sans jamais me sourire en un miroir de poche.

C'est vrai, j'ai bien roulé! j'ai râlé dans des gîtes
Peu vous; mais, n'en ai-je pas plus de mérite
A en avoir sauvé la foi en vos yeux? Dites . . .

– Allons, faisons la paix. Venez, que je vous berce,
Enfant. Eh bien?
                                        – C'est que, votre pardon me verse
Un mélange (confus) d'impressions . . . diverses . . .

(Exit)

My nerves remain responsive to bells, and I'm quite
Fearless and irreproachable when I take the air; you won't catch
Me smiling at myself in a pocket mirror.

I've "experimented," I don't deny, have moaned
And groaned in places where you'd not be seen dead – but surely
Deserve credit for remaining pledged to your eyes . . . "true

To you, darling, in my fashion" . . . so let's make up – come here
And let me cradle you, so . . .
          Oh no! . . . it's just that your forgiveness
Is leaving me more confused than ever . . . prey to different . . .
  to diverse . . .

(Exit)

from
Des Fleurs de Bonne Volonté / Some Flowers of Good Will (1890)

Avertissement

Mon père (un dur par timidité)
Est mort avec un profil sévère;
J'avais presque pas connu ma mère,
Et donc vers vingt ans je suis resté.

Alors, j'ai fait d'la littérature;
Mais le Démon de la Vérité
Sifflotait tout l'temps à mes côtés:
«Pauvre! as-tu fini tes écritures?. . .»

Or, pas le cœur de me marier,
Étant, moi, au fond, trop méprisable!
Et elles pas assez intraitables!
Mais tout l'temps là à s'extasier! . . .

C'est pourquoi je vivotte, vivotte,
Bonne girouette aux trent'-six saisons,
Trop nombreux pour dire oui ou non . . .
– Jeunes gens! que je vous serv' d'Ilote!

Copenhague, Elseneur
1er janvier 1886

Warning

When my father – a shy, stern man –
Died, his features were unrelenting.
I'd barely known my mother.
I was nearing twenty.

So I took up writing . . . but I kept
Hearing that Demon *Truth*
Whistling over my efforts: "These effusions,
My dear boy . . . really . . . have you not done?"

I hadn't the heart to get married, feeling
For myself only bitter contempt.
And *they* proved real sticklers – in-
Flexible – however much they seemed to be in ecstasy!

Which is why I gad about, dither, somehow
Survive, a weather vane buffeted by the thirty-six seasons,
Too many for me to cope with . . . Take heed, I say,
Of my dismal example, O youth of today!

Copenhagen, Elsinore,
1st January 1886

Romance

HAMLET: To a nunnery, go.

J'ai mille oiseaux de mer d'un gris pâle,
Qui nichent au haut de ma belle âme,
Ils en emplissent les tristes salles
De rythmes pris aux plus fines lames . . .

Or, ils salissent tout de charognes,
Et aussi de coraux, de coquilles;
Puis volent en ronds fous, et se cognent
A mes probes lambris de famille . . .

Oiseaux pâles, oiseaux des sillages!
Quand la fiancée ouvrira la porte,
Faites un collier des coquillages
Et que l'odeur de charogn's soit forte! . . .

Qu'Elle dise: «Cette âme est bien forte
«Pour mon petit nez . . . – je me r'habille.
«Mais ce beau collier? hein, je l'emporte?
«Il ne lui sert de rien, pauvre fille . . .»

Romance

HAMLET: To a nunnery, go.

I've a thousand seabirds nesting in the upper reaches
Of my soul. They're pale and grey, and fill
The dismal rooms
With rhythms sharp as waves, as knives . . .

They dirty everywhere with carcases,
With corals, seashells . . . Circling
Crazily, they crash into each other
And into the bourgeois wainscotting of my soul.

Pale birds, you who follow in the wake
Of ships – when my fiancée opens
The door, make for her a necklace
Of shellfish, one that stinks of carrion.

At which she will observe: "This soul is rather
Too strong for my little nose – so I think not.
But this beautiful necklace – can I keep it?"
. . . Ah, poor thing, it will do her no good . . .

Dimanches

HAMLET: Have you a daughter?
POLONIUS: I have, my lord.
HAMLET: Let her not walk i' the sun; conception is a blessing; but not as your daughter may conceive.

Le ciel pleut sans but, sans que rien l'émeuve –
Il pleut, il pleut, bergère! sur le fleuve . . .

Le fleuve a son repos dominical;
Pas un chaland, en amont, en aval.

Les Vêpres carillonnent sur la ville.
Les berges sont désertes, sans idylles.

Passe un pensionnat (ô pauvres chairs!)
Plusieurs ont déjà leurs manchons d'hiver.

Une qui n'a ni manchon, ni fourrures,
Fait, tout en gris, une bien pauv' figure.

Et la voilà qui s'échappe des rangs,
Et court! ô mon Dieu, qu'est-ce qu'il lui prend!

Et elle va se jeter dans le fleuve.
Pas un batelier, pas un chien Terr' Neuve.

Sundays

HAMLET: Have you a daughter?
POLONIUS: I have, my lord.
HAMLET: Let her not walk i' the sun: conception is a blessing;
but not as your daughter may conceive.

Rain, pointless rain, emotionless rain
Falls into the river – *il pleut, il pleut bergère.*

Sunday is a rest day for the river –
Not a barge moves upstream or down.

Vespers rings out over town;
The banks are deserted, dispiriting.

Girls from the local boarding school pass (oh how deeply
I pity them!) some already wearing their winter muffs.

One, who has neither muff nor furs, and is dressed
All in grey, seems particularly miserable.

Suddenly she breaks ranks – and runs –
Oh my God! – what's got into her?

She's going to throw herself into the river!
And there's not a boatman, not a rescue dog in sight!

Le crépuscule vient; le petit port
Allume ses feux. (Ah! connu, l'décor!)

La pluie continue à mouiller le fleuve,
Le ciel pleut sans but, sans que rien l'émeuve.

Night falls, and the little port
Is lit up (Ah, it's all

So recognizable!). And the rain drenches
The river, pointless, emotionless.

Avant-dernier mot

L'Espace?
– Mon Cœur
Y meurt
Sans traces . . .

En vérité, du haut des terrasses,
Tout est bien sans cœur.

La Femme?
– J'en sors,
La mort
Dans l'âme . . .

En vérité, mieux ensemble on pâme
Moins on est d'accord.

Le Rêve?
– C'est bon
Quand on
L'achève . . .

En vérité, la Vie est bien brève,
Le Rêve bien long.

Almost Last Word

Space? There
My heart
Fails – leaves
No trace.

Even aloft on some sky-
High terrace, believe me, all is heartless.

Women? I'm
Off – can-can-
Cankered
In soul.

The deeper, I swear, the shared swoon, the more
Fractious the *ree-lay-shun-ship.*

Dreams? They're
Best by far
Once over
And done with.

Life, I tell you, flies by, but dreams
Are stubborn, refuse to die.

Que faire
Alors
Du corps
Qu'on gère?

En vérité, ô mes ans, que faire
De ce riche corps?

Ceci,
Cela,
Par-ci
Par-là . . .

En vérité, en vérité, voilà,
Et pour le reste, que Tout m'ait en sa merci.

So, my obedient
Body, what USE
Can be made
Of you?

Oh yes, o years, how get the very best from this
Top of the range body? Try:

This one,
That one,
This way,
That way . . .

It's true, it's true – it is.
And for the rest, may All That Exists have pity on me.

Les chauves-souris

C'est qu'elles m'ont l'air bien folles, ce soir,
Les cloches du couvent des carmélites!
Et je me demande au nom de quels rites . . .
Allons, montons voir.

Oh! parmi les poussiéreuses poutrelles,
Ce sont de jeunes chauves-souris
Folles d'essayer enfin hors du nid
Leurs vieillottes ailes!

– Elles s'en iront désormais aux soirs,
Chasser les moustiques sur la rivière,
A l'heure où les diurnes lavandières
Ont tu leurs battoirs.

– Et ces couchants seront tout solitaires,
Tout quotidiens et tout supra-Védas,
Tout aussi vrais que si je n'étais pas,
Tout à leur affaire.

Ah! ils seront tout aussi quotidiens
Qu'aux temps où la planète à la dérive
En ses langes de vapeurs primitives
Ne savait rien d'rien.

The Bats

It's because they seem so frenzied this evening, the bells
Of the Carmelite Convent . . . what rite
I wonder, can they be ringing for? *Allons,*
        Let's up and see . . .

Goodness! Among the dusty beams
Are bats, young ones, eager
To test-fly outside the nest their antique
        Wings . . .

From now on, each evening, they'll be hunting
Mosquitoes down by the river, at just the hour
When the laundry women stop pounding
        Their washing . . .

And these sunsets will be a quintessence
Of loneliness, wholly ordinary and yet supra-
Vedic, will keep on happening on their own terms, regardless
        Of me.

Yes, they'll be forever the same
As when this drifting planet was in
Its infancy, swaddled in primitive mists,
        And knew nothing.

Ils seront tout aussi à leur affaire
Quand je ne viendrai plus crier bravo!
Aux assortiments de mourants joyaux
          De leur éventaire,

Qu'aux jours où certain bohème filon
Du commun néant n'avait pas encore
Pris un accès d'existence pécore
          Sous mon pauvre nom.

And they'll happen just this way when I
Am no longer here to exclaim "Bravo!"
At the glowing, fading colours spread out like jewels
        On a market tray –

Occur exactly as before an unstable
Compound of the banal and vacant assumed
Its boobyish existence under my
        Pitiful name.

Derniers Vers / Last Poems (1890)

I have not art to reckon my groans thine evermore,
most dear lady, whilst this machine is to him.

J.L.

OPHELIA: He took me by the wrist, and held me hard;
Then goes he to the length of all his arm,
And, with his other hand thus o'er his brow,
He falls to such perusal of my face,
As he would draw it. Long stay'd he so:
At last, – a little shaking of mine arm,
And thrice his head thus waving up and down,
He rais'd a sigh so piteous and profound,
That it did seem to shatter all his bulk,
And end his being. That done he lets me go,
And with his head over his shoulder turn'd
He seem'd to find his way without his eyes;
For out o'doors he went without their help,
And to the last bended their light on me.
POLONIUS: This is the very ecstasy of love.

(I)

L'hiver qui vient

Blocus sentimental! Messageries du Levant! . . .
Oh, tombée de la pluie! Oh! tombée de la nuit,
Oh! le vent! . . .
La Toussaint, la Noël et la Nouvelle Année,
Oh, dans les bruines, toutes mes cheminées! . . .
D'usines . . .

On ne peut plus s'asseoir, tous les bancs sont mouillés;
Crois-moi, c'est bien fini jusqu'à l'année prochaine,
Tant les bancs sont mouillés, tant les bois sont rouillés,
Et tant les cors ont fait ton ton, ont fait ton taine! . . .

Ah, nuées accourues des côtes de la Manche,
Vous nous avez gâté notre dernier dimanche.

Il bruine;
Dans la forêt mouillée, les toiles d'araignées
Ploient sous les gouttes d'eau, et c'est leur ruine.

Soleils plénipotentiaires des travaux en blonds Pactoles
Des spectacles agricoles,

(I)

The Coming of Winter

Sentimental blockade! – Levantine
Shipping lines! . . . Rain
Falling, night
Falling – and wind. All
Saints Day, Christmas Day, New Year's Day . . . drizzle,
Chimneys, chimneys
Factory chimneys . . .

One can't sit down
Because the benches are wet; now everything's
Over until next year. The benches are wet
And the wood
Mildewed, because the horns
Have sounded *ton ton, ton taine*!

Clouds hurrying from the English Channel have ruined
Our final Sunday.

Drizzle:
In the dripping forest spiderwebs sway
Under beads of water, are undone
By them. So where

Have you interred, O puissant sun, the Pactolian streams
That should be bathing in golden

Où êtes-vous ensevelis?
Ce soir un soleil fichu gît au haut du coteau
Gît sur le flanc, dans les genêts, sur son manteau,
Un soleil blanc comme un crachat d'estaminet
Sur une litière de jaunes genêts
De jaunes genêts d'automne.
Et les cors lui sonnent!
Qu'il revienne . . .
Qu'il revienne à lui!
Taïaut! Taïaut! et hallali!
Ô triste antienne, as-tu fini! . . .
Et font les fous! . . .
Et il gît là, comme une glande arrachée dans un cou,
Et il frissonne, sans personne! . . .

Allons, allons, et hallali!
C'est l'Hiver bien connu qui s'amène;
Oh! les tournants des grandes routes,
Et sans petit Chaperon Rouge qui chemine! . . .
Oh! leurs ornières des chars de l'autre mois,
Montant en don quichottesques rails
Vers les patrouilles des nuées en déroute
Que le vent malmène vers les transatlantiques bercails! . . .
Accélérons, accélérons, c'est la saison bien connue, cette fois.

Et le vent, cette nuit, il en a fait de belles!
Ô dégâts, ô nids, ô modestes jardinets!
Mon cœur et mon sommeil: ô échos des cognées! . . .

Bucolic light a farmer's crops and fields? Cloaked
And scarfed is the lousy sun that lies across the hill's
Flank, in the gorse, this evening . . . this sun's as white
Against the autumn's sprawling yellow gorse
As a gobbet of spit on the floor
Of an estaminet . . . and now the horns
Are summoning him to return, to return
To himself – *Taïaut! Taïaut!*
Hallali! O sad refrain, are you
Not done yet? Crazy crazy hullaballoo! And there
The sun lies, like a gland torn from a neck, shuddering, alone . . .

Let's go, let's go, tallyho, *hallali!*
For winter, known to all, is fast
Approaching. Down
The turnings off the main roads no Little
Red Riding Hood makes her way . . . the ruts left
By wagons last month are Don Quixote-style rails stretching
Into the sky where the wind drives
Scattered squadrons of clouds towards their trans-
Atlantic sheepfolds . . . well-known
Season, faster, faster – oh the wind, this night
Has cut a swathe . . . nests, humble gardens, wreckage . . .
Oh my heart, my sleep . . . echoes, echoes of falling
Axes . . .

Tous ces rameaux avaient encor leurs feuilles vertes,
Les sous-bois ne sont plus qu'un fumier de feuilles mortes;
Feuilles, folioles, qu'un bon vent vous emporte
Vers les étangs par ribambelles,
Ou pour le feu du garde-chasse,
Ou les sommiers des ambulances
Pour les soldats loin de la France.

C'est la saison, c'est la saison, la rouille envahit les masses,
La rouille ronge en leurs spleens kilométriques
Les fils télégraphiques des grandes routes où nul ne passe.

Les cors, les cors, les cors – mélancoliques! . . .
Mélancoliques! . . .
S'en vont, changeant de ton,
Changeant de ton et de musique,
Ton ton, ton taine, ton ton! . . .
Les cors, les cors, les cors! . . .
S'en sont allés au vent du Nord.

Je ne puis quitter ce ton: que d'échos! . . .
C'est la saison, c'est la saison, adieu vendanges! . . .
Voici venir les pluies d'une patience d'ange,
Adieu vendanges, et adieu tous les paniers,
Tous les paniers Watteau des bourrées sous les marronniers,
C'est la toux dans les dortoirs du lycée qui rentre,
C'est la tisane sans le foyer,
La phtisie pulmonaire attristant le quartier,
Et toute la misère des grands centres.

There were green leaves on these branches . . .
Now the undergrowth is just a mulch of rotting foliage.
Leaves and leaflets, may a strong wind
Sweep you in droves to the lake,
To the game-keeper's fire, to the pallets used
In ambulances by soldiers
Far from France.

It's that time of year – rust
Colours are everywhere, rust gnawing the telegraph wires
Drooping mile after dreary mile
Beside the highways where no one walks.

The horns, the horns . . . mournful,
Melancholy . . . they depart
And return, their timbre
Altered . . . *ton ton, ton taine, ton ton!*
The horns – the horns have departed
With the north wind.

I cannot escape the note
They sound, nor their echoes . . . it's the season's
Fault – farewell
Vendanges . . . in their stead, rains that evoke the patience
Of angels . . . farewell *vendanges*, and baskets
Like those in a *fête champêtre* by Watteau, dances
Under the chestnut trees . . . in their stead, coughing
In the boarding school dormitory at night, and tisane served
Far from home . . . tuberculosis saddening
The *quartier*, the endless
Sorrows afflicting the great cities.

Mais, lainages, caoutchoucs, pharmacie, rêve,
Rideaux écartés du haut des balcons des grèves
Devant l'océan de toitures des faubourgs,
Lampes, estampes, thé, petits-fours,
Serez-vous pas mes seules amours! . . .
(Oh! et puis, est-ce que tu connais, outre les pianos,
Le sobre et vespéral mystère hebdomadaire
Des statistiques sanitaires
Dans les journaux?)

Non, non! C'est la saison et la planète falote!
Que l'autan, que l'autan
Effiloche les savates que le Temps se tricote!
C'est la saison, oh déchirements! c'est la saison!
Tous les ans, tous les ans,
J'essaierai en chœur d'en donner la note.

Woollen and waterproof garments, the dispensary,
A dream, curtains parted
Above a strip of balconies overlooking
A sea of suburban roofs . . . lamps, prints, tea,
Petits-fours . . . *you* will have to be
My only loves . . . (Then again – as well as
The pianos – there's the unshowy, twilit mystery
Of the medical statistics issued week
By week in the newspapers . . .)

No no – blame the season and this
Droll planet! Let the southerly wind unravel
The worn-out slippers Time knits for herself!
Oh the season, the season – the rending,
The heartbreak. . . each year
I will endeavour, like a Greek chorus, to sound
The season's particular
Note . . .

(II)

Le mystère des trois cors

Un cor dans la plaine
Souffle à perdre haleine,
Un autre, du fond des bois,
Lui répond;
L'un chante ton-taine
Aux forêts prochaines,
Et l'autre ton-ton
Aux échos des monts.

Celui de la plaine
Sent gonfler ses veines,
Ses veines du front;
Celui du bocage,
En vérité, ménage
Ses jolis poumons.

– Où donc tu te caches,
Mon beau cor de chasse?
Que tu es méchant!

– Je cherche ma belle,
Là-bas, qui m'appelle
Pour voir le Soleil couchant.

(II)

The Mystery of the Three Horns

On the plain there's a horn
Blowing, blowing, while another
From the depths of the wood
Responds: one sings *ton taine*
To the neighbouring
Forests, the other *ton ton*
To the echoing crags.

The horn of the plain
Can feel the veins
On its forehead expand; that
Of the woodland is cannier,
Demands less of the lungs.

"So where are you hiding
My fine hunting horn? How
Naughty you're being!"

"I'm seeking my beloved
Who is calling me, calling me
To view with her the setting sun."

– Taïaut! Taïaut! Je t'aime!
Hallali! Roncevaux!

– Etre aimé est bien doux;
Mais, le Soleil qui se meurt, avant tout!

Le Soleil dépose sa pontificale étole,
Lâche les écluses du Grand-Collecteur
En mille Pactoles
Que les plus artistes
De nos liquoristes
Attisent de cent fioles de vitriol oriental! . . .
Le sanglant étang, aussitôt s'étend, aussitôt s'étale,
Noyant les cavales du quadrige
Qui se cabre, et qui patauge, et puis se fige
Dans ces déluges de bengale et d'alcool! . . .

Mais les durs sables et les cendres de l'horizon
Ont vite bu tout cet étalage des poisons.

Ton-ton ton-taine, les gloires! . . .

Et les cors consternés
Se retrouvent nez à nez;
Ils sont trois;
Le vent se lève, il commence à faire froid.

Ton-ton ton-taine, les gloires! . . .

'*Taïaut! Taïaut!* I love you!
Hallali! Roncevaux!"

"Being loved is sweet; but the sun's
Dying must come first."

The sun lays down its papal stole,
Opens the sluices on the main drain, releasing
A thousand golden streams that the most
Aesthetically inclined of our wine
And spirit merchants stir into flame with a hundred
Flasks of eastern vitriol.
At once the blood-drenched pool begins to spread
And spread, swamping the mares pulling
The chariot that bucks and flounders and ends
Up mired in floods of alcohol and shooting flames.

But the hard sands and ashes of the horizon
Have rapidly absorbed this parade of toxins.

Ton ton ton taine, les gloires! . . .

Disconcerted, the horns
Find themselves nose
To nose, again.

They are three;
The wind rises – it's beginning to grow cold.

Ton ton ton taine, les gloires!

– «Bras-dessus, bras-dessous,
«Avant de rentrer chacun chez nous,
«Si nous allions boire
«Un coup?»

Pauvres cors! pauvres cors!
Comme ils dirent cela avec un rire amer!
(Je les entends encor).

Le lendemain, l'hôtesse du *Grand-Saint-Hubert*
Les trouva tous trois morts.

On fut quérir les autorités
De la localité,

Qui dressèrent procès-verbal
De ce mystère très-immoral.

"Arm in arm . . . arm in arm . . . before
Heading home – a drink?"

Poor horns! poor horns! – that said
With a bitter laugh (I hear them still).

The next day, the landlady of the *Grand-*
Saint-Hubert found all three dead.

The authorities
Of the region were sent for – and duly

Issued a report on this highly
Immoral mystery.

(III)

Dimanches

Bref, j'allais me donner d'un «Je vous aime»
Quand je m'avisai non sans peine
Que d'abord je ne me possédais pas bien moi-même.

(Mon Moi, c'est Galathée aveuglant Pygmalion!
Impossible de modifier cette situation.)

Ainsi donc, pauvre, pâle et piètre individu
Qui ne croit à son Moi qu'à ses moments perdus,
Je vis s'effacer ma fiancée
Emportée par le cours des choses,
Telle l'épine voit s'effeuiller,
Sous prétexte de soir sa meilleure rose.

Or, cette nuit anniversaire, toutes les Walkyries du vent
Sont revenues beugler par les fentes de ma porte:
Væ soli!
Mais, ah! qu'importe?
Il fallait m'en étourdir avant!
Trop tard! ma petite folie est morte!
Qu'importe *Væ soli!*
Je ne retrouverai plus ma petite folie.

(III)

Sundays

I was, in short, on the point
Of handing over my "inner self
With an "I love you" when a dispiriting
Thought occurred to me – I had no "inner self"
To hand over . . .

("Inner self!" . . . imagine Galatea dazzling
Pygmalion – or some such impossible situation.)

A feeble, pale, inadequate type
Crippled by an unstable
And erratic sense of self – *c'est moi!* I watched
My fiancée drift away on the tides
Of life – as a rose-bush watches
Its finest blossom unpetal in the gloaming.

Now the Valkyries
Of the wind are trumpeting through my ill-
Fitting door this anniversary night – *Væ soli!* – *Woe
To him that is alone.* It barely
Matters – I should have
Numbed myself to it before . . . too late . . .
My little foolish fantasy is dead – *Væ soli!* I'll
Never recover *ma petite folie.*

Le grand vent bâillonné,
S'endimanche enfin le ciel du matin.
Et alors, eh! allez donc, carillonnez,
Toutes cloches des bons dimanches!
Et passez layettes et collerettes et robes blanches
Dans un frou-frou de lavande et de thym
Vers l'encens et les brioches!
Tout pour la famille, quoi! *Væ soli!* C'est certain.

La jeune demoiselle à l'ivoirin paroissien
Modestement rentre au logis.
On le voit, son petit corps bien reblanchi
Sait qu'il appartient
A un tout autre passé que le mien!

Mon corps, ô ma sœur, a bien mal à sa belle âme . . .

Oh! voilà que ton piano
Me recommence, si natal maintenant!
Et ton cœur qui s'ignore s'y ânonne
En ritournelles de bastringues à tout venant,
Et ta pauvre chair s'y fait mal! . . .
A moi, Walkyries!
Walkyries des hypocondries et des tueries!

Ah, que je te les tordrais avec plaisir,
Ce corps bijou, ce cœur à ténor,
Et te dirais leur fait, et puis encore
La manière de s'en servir

The morning sky at last emerges
In its Sunday best, the screaming winds
Now muzzled – ye Sunday bells, ring out!
Loud and clear! – and chivvy the procession
Of layettes and lace collars and white dresses, amid
The rustling of lavender and thyme, towards the incense
And brioches! Family values, eh? *Woe*
To him that is alone!

Modestly returning home clutching an ivory-bound
Prayerbook, a young *demoiselle* . . . One
Can tell her fastidiously
Scrubbed body knows her history
Separates her utterly from me.

Sister, my lofty soul aches, and my body
Feels it . . .

At which point your piano
Triggers me, has me feeling all
Indigenous . . . in its blithe way your heart
Stumbles through show tunes and ritornellos to all
Comers – and oh how your poor flesh
Suffers . . . Valkyries! Valkyries! Descend
On me, you agents of hypochondrias, of massacres!

With what pleasure I would wring
Both your precious body and your tenor's
Heart, outline to you the point of them, and what use
Should be made of them, by you –

De s'en servir à deux,
Si tu voulais seulement m'approfondir ensuite un peu!

Non, non! C'est sucer la chair d'un cœur élu,
Adorer d'incurables organes
S'entrevoir avant que les tissus se fanent
En monomanes, en reclus!

Et ce n'est pas sa chair qui me serait tout,
Et je ne serais pas qu'un grand cœur pour elle,
Mais quoi s'en aller faire les fous
Dans des histoires fraternelles!
L'âme et la chair, la chair et l'âme,
C'est l'esprit édénique et fier
D'être un peu l'Homme avec la Femme.

En attendant, oh! garde-toi des coups de tête,
Oh! file ton rouet et prie et reste honnête.

– Allons, dernier des poètes,
Toujours enfermé tu te rendras malade!
Vois, il fait beau temps, tout le monde est dehors,
Va donc acheter deux sous d'ellébore,
Ça te fera une petite promenade.

By us . . . and oh! if only afterwards
Your interest in *me* grew deeper, were enhanced!

No, no . . . to tongue the flesh of a heart
Elect, to adore
With incurable organs? . . . to glimpse
Each other before our living tissue dissolves
In solipsism, in monomania . . .

Now you're not to think I'm obsessed with her body
Nor ditzy in a spiritual-soulmate sort of way – as if
It were worth making fools
Of ourselves to be "sister and brother".
Body and soul, soul and body . . . proud Adam
And Eve in the garden of Eden suggest
A little how a man might be with a woman . . .

And while we wait, beware the sudden rush of blood
To the head! Keep on at your spinning-wheel, keep saying
Your prayers, and above all
Keep honest . . .

"Listen, worst of poets, you'll make
Yourself ill, shut up all day! *Tout
le monde* is on the streets, outdoors, and the weather's
Glorious: go buy yourself two *sous*'
Worth of hellebore – a little promenade
Might do you good."

(IV)

Dimanches

C'est l'automne, l'automne, l'automne,
Le grand vent et toute sa séquelle
De représailles! et de musiques! . . .
Rideaux tirés, clôture annuelle,
Chute des feuilles, des Antigones, des Philomèles:
Mon fossoyeur, *Alas poor Yorick!*
Les remue à la pelle! . . .

Vivent l'Amour et les feux de paille! . . .

Les Jeunes Filles inviolables et frêles
Descendent vers la petite chapelle
Dont les chimériques cloches
Du joli joli dimanche
Hygiéniquement et élégamment les appellent.

Comme tout se fait propre autour d'elles!
Comme tout en est dimanche!

Comme on se fait dur et boudeur à leur approche! . . .

Ah! moi, je demeure l'Ours Blanc!
Je suis venu par ces banquises
Plus pures que les communiantes en blanc . . .

(IV)

Sundays

It's autumn – autumn – autumn –
Which means gusting winds and their
Aftermath . . . music, drawn curtains, annual closures, falling
Antigones and leaves and Philomels . . . My own
Gravedigger (*Alas poor Yorick!*) stirs
Them with his spade.

Vive l'Amour – and long live
Whatever is only
A flash in the pan . . .

On this charming charming Sunday, fantastical
Church bells summon
Oh so elegantly, so
Hygienically, frail, inviolable
Jeunes Filles to the little chapel.

They converge in an aura
Of cleanliness, of Sundayness . . . and I

Turn stony and sullen at their approach, feel
Again like a polar bear
Who has travelled over icefloes whiter
Than the white

Moi, je ne vais pas à l'église,
Moi, je suis le Grand Chancelier de l'Analyse,
Qu'on se le dise.

Pourtant, pourtant! Qu'est-ce que c'est que cette anémie?
Voyons, confiez vos chagrins à votre vieil ami . . .

Vraiment! Vraiment!
Ah! Je me tourne vers la mer, les éléments
Et tout ce qui n'a plus que les noirs grognements!

Oh! que c'est sacré!
Et qu'il y faut de grandes veillées!

Pauvre, pauvre, sous couleur d'attraits! . . .

Et nous, et nous,
Ivres, ivres, avant qu'émerveillés . . .
Qu'émerveillés et à genoux! . . .

Et voyez comme on tremble
Au premier grand soir
Que tout pousse au désespoir
D'en mourir ensemble!

Ô merveille qu'on n'a su que cacher!
Si pauvre et si brûlante et si martyre!

Of their communion dresses . . . and I, who do not
Attend church, issue this
Warning: I am the Master, the Lord
High Chancellor
Of ANALYSIS!

What's this! You suffer
From anaemia? Come, come, tell your old pal all!

Indeed, the groaning of the sea, lamentations, and nature's
Darker elements are all
That appeal to me! . . .

How "sacred" it is – but the vigilance
Required, the *nuits blanches*! . . .

Seems appealing – but underneath, a poor thing . . .

While we
Get drunk, then astounded,
And astounded, kneel . . .

All aquiver that first, decisive
Evening, as if gripped by desperate fear
Of dying of it, together . . .

Impoverished . . . aflame . . . martyrish . . .
Wonder that had to be kept hidden –

Et qu'on n'ose toucher
Qu'à l'aveugle, en divin délire!

Ô merveille,
Reste cachée idéale violette,
L'Univers te veille,
Les générations de planètes te tettent,
De funérailles en relevailles! . . .

Oh, que c'est plus haut
Que ce Dieu et que la Pensée!
Et rien qu'avec ces chers yeux en haut
Tout inconscients et couleurs de pensée! . . .
Si frêle, si frêle!
Et tout le mortel foyer
Tout, tout ce foyer en elle! . . .

Oh, pardonnez-lui si, malgré elle,
Et cela tant lui sied,
Parfois ses prunelles clignent un peu
Pour vous demander un peu
De vous apitoyer un peu!

Ô frêle, frêle, et toujours prête
Pour ces messes dont on a fait un jeu
Penche, penche ta chère tête, va,
Regarde les grappes des premiers lilas,
Il ne s'agit pas de conquêtes, avec moi,
Mais d'au-delà!

Is only to be touched, eyes
Tight shut, in a divine frenzy . . .

O remain secret, miraculous
Perfect violet, the universe watches
Over you – and planet
After planet will suckle you . . . from funerals
To churchings . . .

It o'erleaps both
God and Thinking . . . and does so
Using its own dear eyes, unselfconscious,
Uplifted, the colour of thought . . .
So frail, so frail . . . and the seat
Of the world itself
Wrapped up in her . . .

Now if, to arouse your pity, and despite
Herself, on occasion she flutters
Her eyelashes
A little, in a becoming manner, you must
Forgive her . . .

Frail, frail, always ready
For mass, regardless of our
Mockery, bend your dear head, and consider
These clusters of early lilacs . . . it's no longer, for me,
A question of 'winning' but of whatever
Is beyond . . .

Oh! puissions-nous quitter la vie
Ensemble dès cette Grand'Messe,
Écœurés de notre espèce
Qui bâille assouvie
Dès le parvis! . . .

The Grand Mass over, swarms of churchgoers, smug
And yawning, fill the square . . . *ugh* . . . if only
We could exit *à deux*, leave them
(And life) behind
Forever . . .

(V)

Pétition

Amour absolu, carrefour sans fontaine;
Mais, à tous les bouts, d'étourdissantes fêtes foraines.

Jamais franches,
Ou le poing sur la hanche:
Avec toutes, l'amour s'échange
Simple et sans foi comme un bonjour.

Ô bouquets d'oranger cuirassés de satin,
Elle s'éteint, elle s'éteint,
La divine Rosace
A voir vos noces de sexes livrés à la grosse,
Courir en valsant vers la fosse
Commune! . . . Pauvre race!

Pas d'absolu; des compromis;
Tout est pas plus, tout est permis.

Et cependant, ô des nuits, laissez-moi, Circés,
Sombrement coiffées à la Titus,
Et les yeux en grand deuil comme des pensées!

(V)

Petition

Absolute love
Equals a fountainless junction – from which raucous, festive
Funfairs can be heard
In all directions . . .

Hand on hip, never, any of them,
Candid, they make
Of love no more
Than a fleeting exchange, a casual *bonjour.*

O bouquets of orange-blossom
Armoured in satin – the light filtering
From on high, through the divine
Rose-window is dimming, dimming . . . couple
After couple waltz to the altar, to the marriage bed, towards
The common grave . . . Ah, humanity!

The absolute
Has been jettisoned, and compromise ("No further . . . permission
Granted . . .") reigns.

Sisters of Circe, with your hair gloomily curled
Like that of the Roman Emperor Titus, with your eyes
Dark as pansies as if sunk

Et passez,
Béatifiques Vénus
Étalées et découvrant vos gencives comme un régal,
Et bâillant des aisselles au soleil
Dans l'assourdissement des cigales!
Ou, droites, tenant sur fond violet le lotus
Des sacrilèges domestiques,
En faisant de l'index: *motus!*

Passez, passez, bien que les yeux vierges
Ne soient que cadrans d'émail bleu,
Marquant telle heure que l'on veut,
Sauf à garder pour eux, pour Elle,
Leur heure immortelle.
Sans doute au premier mot,
On va baisser ces yeux,
Et peut-être choir en syncope,
On est si vierge à fleur de robe
Peut-être même à fleur de peau,
Mais leur destinée est bien interlope, au nom de Dieu!

Ô historiques esclaves!
Oh! leur petite chambre!
Qu'on peut les en faire descendre
Vers d'autres étages,
Vers les plus frelatées des caves,
Vers les moins ange-gardien des ménages!

In mourning, when night
Falls, let me be . . . and ignore
Me too, you descendants
Of Venus the Beatific, lounging, proffering a glimpse
Of your gums as a treat or displaying
Your armpits to the sun amid the din
Of mating crickets . . . or stiffly upright against
A violet background, cradling the symbolic lotus of life-
Quenching domesticity, index finger raised
To the lips demanding: QUIET!

What if – pass on, pass on – you see
In an innocent eye the glazed
Blue dial of a clock that tells
Whatever time you want . . . it is, remember,
Her "immortal hour" that those eyes, and she,
Are guarding. She will, it goes
Without saying, instantly lower her gaze at the first
Word – and might even swoon
At the same time . . . and while "Virginity" is signalled
By dress, or even skin-tones, the future
That looms, O Lord, is . . . well, not exactly salubrious.

Slaves of history . . . think
Of their little bedrooms, from which, floor
By floor, you can make them descend . . . and of the common
Basement where they end up, performing tasks
Or roles no one could call
Angelic . . .

Et alors, le grand Suicide, à froid,
Et leur *Amen* d'une voix sans Elle,
Tout en vaquant aux petits soins secrets,
Et puis leur éternel air distrait
Leur grand air de dire: «De quoi?»
«Ah! de quoi, au fond, s'il vous plaît?»

Mon Dieu, que l'Idéal
La dépouillât de ce rôle d'ange!
Qu'elle adoptât l'Homme comme égal!
Oh, que ses yeux ne parlent plus d'Idéal,
Mais simplement d'humains échanges!
En frère et sœur par le cœur,
Et fiancés par le passé,
Et puis unis par l'Infini!
Oh, simplement d'infinis échanges
A la fin de journées
A quatre bras moissonnées,
Quand les tambours, quand les trompettes,
Ils s'en vont sonnant la retraite,
Et qu'on prend le frais sur le pas des portes,
En vidant les pots de grès
A la santé des années mortes
Qui n'ont pas laissé de regrets,
Au su de tout le canton
Que depuis toujours nous habitons,
Ton ton, ton taine, ton ton.

What follows? Dispassionate self-
Annihilation, each *Amen* murmured
Automatically, insistent juggling of private niggles
And worries, endless distrac[illegible] *nat? What's*
That? . . . whatever . . . whatever . . . whatever. . ."

Mon Dieu – if only the "Ideal"
Itself could release women from the notion
They are angels! . . . in fact, when the "Ideal" animates
Their eyes, it merely destroys the chance of engaging
As equals, in the manner, say, of affectionate siblings
Linked by their history,
By their boundless
Future . . . what I envisage, at the end
Of a shared, well-used day, as trumpets and drums sound
Its retreat, is easy-going companionship . . . O picture
Us taking the air on our doorstep, emptying
Earthenware jugs in honour of the happy
Passing years we've spent as model citizens
In this neighbourhood where we've lived
Forever . . . ha-ha . . . ho-ho . . . ha-ha . . . *ton ton,*
Ton taine, ton ton.

(VI)

Simple agonie

Ô paria! – Et revoici les sympathies de mai.
Mais tu ne peux que te répéter, ô honte!
Et tu te gonfles et ne crèves jamais.
Et tu sais fort bien, ô paria,
Que ce n'est pas du tout ça.

Oh! que
Devinant l'instant le plus seul de la nature,
Ma mélodie, toute et unique, monte,
Dans le soir et redouble, et fasse tout ce qu'elle peut
Et dise la chose qu'est la chose,
Et retombe, et reprenne,
Et fasse de la peine,
Ô solo de sanglots,
Et reprenne et retombe
Selon la tâche qui lui incombe.
Oh! que ma musique
Se crucifie,
Selon sa photographie
Accoudée et mélancolique! . . .

Il faut trouver d'autres thèmes,
Plus mortels et plus suprêmes.

(VI)

Simple Agony

May, O pariah, is here
Again, sympathetic May . . . and shame, reciting itself
Like a litany, swelling and swelling –
Never bursting . . . and yet, as you know
So well, pariah, *that* is not it at all . . .

How I wish my song
Could chance upon the very essence of solitude, could rise
At evening, unique and whole, endowed
With doubled powers and determined to say what *this*
Thing is . . . then die
Away, only to gather strength
Again, become
A sobbing aria, source
Of pain, now rising now falling as if
Obeying some pre-
Determined plan . . . and oh for my song
To be self-crucifying, to match this photograph
Of her, leaning on her elbows, in thrall
To melancholy . . .

Other, more elevated, life-and-death themes
Must be found, this world being

Oh! bien, avec le monde tel quel,
Je vais me faire un monde plus mortel!

Les âmes y seront à musique,
Et tous les intérêts puérilement charnels,
Ô fanfares dans les soirs,
Ce sera barbare,
Ce sera sans espoir.

Enquêtes, enquêtes,
Seront l'unique fête!
Qui m'en défie?
J'entasse sur mon lit, les journaux, linge sale,
Dessins de mode, photographies quelconques,
Toute la capitale,
Matrice sociale.

Que nul n'intercède,
Ce ne sera jamais assez,
Il n'y a qu'un remède,
C'est de tout casser.

Ô fanfares dans les soirs!
Ce sera barbare,
Ce sera sans espoir.
Et nous aurons beau la piétiner à l'envi,
Nous ne serons jamais plus cruels que la vie,
Qui fait qu'il est des animaux injustement rossés,
Et des femmes à jamais laides . . .
Que nul n'intercède,
Il faut tout casser.

What it is . . . try – why not? – imagining
A world beyond

Where souls devote
Themselves to music, where carnality
And childishness are fused, and fanfares fill
The evenings . . .
Primitive . . .
Hopeless . . .

Now let us survey, survey – what harmless
Fun this will be, who could possibly
Not agree? . . . piled on my divan are newspapers, my dirty linen,
Fashion pix, assorted
Photographs – the capital itself, the matrix
Of society . . . interceding
Will neither help nor prove
Worthwhile – just one remedy remains, whole-
Sale destruction.

Fanfares each evening . . .
Primitive . . .
Hopeless . . .
And there's no point, you know, in stamping in rage – we
Can never equal life's cruelty . . . think
Of ill-treated animals, of women
Ugly all their lives . . . no
Interceding . . . whole-
Sale destruction.

Alléluia, Terre paria.
Ce sera sans espoir,
De l'aurore au soir,
Quand il n'y en aura plus il y en aura encore,
Du soir à l'aurore.
Alléluia, Terre paria!
Les hommes de l'art
Ont dit: «Vrai, c'est trop tard.»
Pas de raison,
Pour ne pas activer sa crevaison.

Aux armes, citoyens! Il n'y a plus de RAISON:

Il prit froid l'autre automne,
S'étant attardé vers les peines des cors,
Sur la fin d'un beau jour.
Oh! ce fut pour vos cors, et ce fut pour l'automne,
Qu'il nous montra qu' «on meurt d'amour»!
On ne le verra plus aux fêtes nationales,
S'enfermer dans l'Histoire et tirer les verrous,
Il vint trop tôt, il est reparti sans scandale;
Ô vous qui m'écoutez, rentrez chacun chez vous.

Hallelujah – the Earth itself is a pariah, emptied
Of hope, from dawn to dusk, from dusk
To dawn we empty
Ourselves of hope, only to find
More . . . Hallelujah, earth-pariah! Artistic types
Have asserted, "Hmm, that's true, it's way
Too late" . . . So why delay inflicting
On our era an almighty
Puncture?

Aux armes, citoyens!: There's no more REASON.

The other autumn he caught cold, having stayed
Out late to hear the sorrowing horns – it was for you
O horns, after a splendid day, and for you, O autumn,
That we were shown how one might die
For love. Henceforth, on national holidays, he will not
Be observed drawing the bolts and boxing himself
Into History. He came before
His time, departed without scandal: now you, O you
Who hear me, get yourselves home – *chacun chez vous.*

(VII)

Solo de lune

Je fume, étalé face au ciel,
Sur l'impériale de la diligence,
Ma carcasse est cahotée, mon âme danse
Comme un Ariel;
Sans miel, sans fiel, ma belle âme danse,
Ô routes, coteaux, ô fumées, ô vallons,
Ma belle âme, ah! récapitulons.

Nous nous aimions comme deux fous,
On s'est quitté sans en parler,
Un spleen me tenait exilé,
Et ce spleen me venait de tout. Bon.

Ses yeux disaient: «Comprenez-vous?
«Pourquoi ne comprenez-vous pas?»
Mais nul n'a voulu faire le premier pas,
Voulant trop tomber *ensemble* à genoux.
(Comprenez-vous?)

Où est-elle à cette heure?
Peut-être qu'elle pleure . . .

(VII)

Lunar Solo

I smoke, spread out
Beneath the evening sky on the top-deck
Of a careering stagecoach, every bone
In my body rattling, jangling – but my soul
Is a dancing Ariel, my soul
Whirls beyond bitterness and cloying
Honey, beyond the passing
Roads and hills and valleys and even
My own tobacco fumes . . . and dancing it recalls

That we fell crazily in love . . . and yet we parted
Without mentioning
The fact: spleen drove me away, spleen, all-
Invading spleen.

Her eyes were eloquent: "Do you get it?
Or rather, why oh why do you *not* get it?"
Neither would make
That first move   we had to fall *simultaneously*
Together to our knees,
You see.

Where, I wonder,
Is she now, perhaps crying – where

Où est-elle à cette heure?
Oh! du moins, soigne-toi je t'en conjure!

Ô fraîcheur des bois le long de la route,
Ô châle de mélancolie, toute âme est un peu aux écoutes,
Que ma vie
Fait envie!
Cette impériale de diligence tient de la magie.

Accumulons l'irréparable!
Renchérissons sur notre sort!
Les étoiles sont plus nombreuses que le sable
Des mers où d'autres ont vu se baigner son corps;
Tout n'en va pas moins à la Mort,
Y a pas de port.

Des ans vont passer là-dessus,
On s'endurcira chacun pour soi,
Et bien souvent et déjà je m'y vois,
On se dira: «Si j'avais su . . .»
Mais mariés, de même, ne se fût-on pas dit:
«Si j'avais su, si j'avais su! . . .»!
Ah! rendez-vous maudit!
Ah! mon cœur sans issue! . . .
Je me suis mal conduit.

Maniaques de bonheur,
Donc, que ferons-nous? Moi de mon âme,
Elle de sa faillible jeunesse!

Is she right now? Take care
At any rate, I beg you, do take care.

How cool the woods on either side
Of the road, the road . . . O shawl of melancholy, souls
Are listening, alert – and it's *my*
Life inspiring their envy. Magic
Enfolds the upper deck of this *diligence.*

Let's stockpile whatever can't be fixed, bid
Higher and higher on our fate.
There are more stars than grains of sand
In the seas where others
Have seen her bathing. All slides, as ever, towards
Death, no shelter
From that storm.

The years will skim over all that has happened,
And our hearts
Will harden, apart, leaving us muttering – I can see it
Now – "If only I'd *known* . . ." Married
Or unmarried – "If only, if only
I'd *known* . . ." Accursed be our wretched
Rendezvous! – my heart
Was a sealed box, my behaviour was
. . . not good.

Mad as hatters
For happiness – what on earth
Shall we do now? How can we square my "soul" with her

Ô vieillissante pécheresse,
Oh! que de soirs je vais me rendre infâme
En ton honneur!

Ses yeux clignaient: «Comprenez-vous?
«Pourquoi ne comprenez-vous pas?»
Mais nul n'a fait le premier pas
Pour tomber ensemble à genoux. Ah! . . .

La lune se lève,
Ô route en grand rêve! . . .

On a dépassé les filatures, les scieries,
Plus que les bornes kilométriques,
De petits nuages d'un rose de confiserie,
Cependant qu'un fin croissant de lune se lève.
Ô route de rêve, ô nulle musique . . .
Dans ces bois de pins où depuis
Le commencement du monde
Il fait toujours nuit,
Que de chambres propres et profondes!
Oh! pour un soir d'enlèvement!
Et je les peuple et je m'y vois,
Et c'est un beau couple d'amants,
Qui gesticulent hors la loi.

Et je passe et les abandonne,
Et me recouche face au ciel,
La route tourne, je suis Ariel,

Gullible youth? Must I spend evening
After evening wildly defending – O ageing
Sinner! – your non-
Existent honour.

"Do you" (her eyes
Flashed) "see? How" (her eyes flashed) "can you possibly
Not see?" Yet neither of us took the first step, neither
Fell to our knees.

The moon rises, and the road
Is like a dream . . . we sped

Past cotton-mills and sawmills, but now
Only milestones mark
Our progress, and pink candyfloss clouds
And a frail crescent moon . . . it unfurls, our
Dreamy road, unaccompanied
By music . . . in pinewood forests where night, since time began,
Has reigned, are swept
And secret rooms – to these
One might elope? I people the woods, imagine
Myself in a couple, among handsome lovers escaping
The law . . . excited . . . gesticulating.

And now I
Cast them behind, am Ariel
Himself on this winding road – awaited by no

Nul ne m'attend, je ne vais chez personne.
Je n'ai que l'amitié des chambres d'hôtel!

La lune se lève,
Ô route en grand rêve!
Ô route sans terme,
Voici le relais,
Où l'on allume les lanternes,
Où l'on boit un verre de lait,
Et fouette postillon,
Dans le chant des grillons,
Sous les étoiles de Juillet.

Ô clair de Lune,
Noce de feux de Bengale noyant mon infortune,
Les ombres des peupliers sur la route . . .
Le gave qui s'écoute . . .
Qui s'écoute chanter . . .
Dans ces inondations du fleuve Léthé . . .

Ô solo de lune,
Vous défiez ma plume.
Oh! cette nuit sur la route;
Ô Étoiles, vous êtes à faire peur,
Vous y êtes toutes! toutes!
Ô sagacité de cette heure . . .
Oh! qu'il y eût moyen
De m'en garder l'âme pour l'automne qui vient! . . .

Welcoming host, only the friendship
Of some hotel room.

The moon rises
Above the oneiric, endless
Road – we reach
A staging post, and lighted
Lanterns, a glass of milk, and cries
Of "Drive, postilion,
Drive!" amid chirping
Crickets, beneath the stars
Of July.

My misfortune
Is drowning
In moonlight, in flares like wedding fireworks,
In the shadowy poplars overarching
The road . . . in the song
The mountain torrent
Sings to itself . . . in the rising
Waters of Lethe.

Lunar
Solo, you outwit
My pen, this night
On the road . . . and stars, you scare me, so
Many of you, out there . . . O wisdom
Of the hour – how I wish
I could preserve your inspiration, and draw on it
As autumn looms.

Voici qu'il fait très très frais,
Oh! si à la même heure,
Elle va de même le long des forêts,
Noyer son infortune
Dans ces noces du clair de lune! . . .
(Elle aime tant errer tard!)
Elle aura oublié son foulard,
Elle va prendre mal, vu la beauté de l'heure!
Oh! soigne-toi je t'en conjure!
Oh! Je ne veux plus entendre cette toux!

Ah! que ne suis-je tombé à tes genoux!
Ah! que n'as-tu défailli à mes genoux!
J'eusse été le modèle des époux.
Comme le frou-frou de ta robe est le modèle des frou-frou.

The temperature
Has dropped, and she
May be drifting
Through some forest – she loves
To wander late – drowning
Her sorrows in nuptial moonlight . . . she'll have forgotten
Her scarf and the night's beauties
Will have her rapt in wonder . . . she'll catch cold, oh please
Take care – what I would give never again to have to hear
Your coughing.

Once more – why oh why oh why did we fail
To tumble, fainting, at each other's feet! I would have been
The paragon of spouses – just as no froufrou could ever match
The froufrou made by your dress
When you move.

(VIII)

Légende

Armorial d'anémie!
Psautier d'automne!
Offertoire de tout mon ciboire de bonheur et de génie,
A cette hostie si féminine,
Et si petite toux sèche maligne,
Qu'on voit aux jours déserts, en inconnue,
Sertie en de cendreuses toilettes qui sentent déjà l'hiver,
Se fuir le long des cris surhumains de la Mer.

Grandes amours, oh! qu'est-ce encor! . . .

En tout cas, des lèvres sans façon,
Des lèvres déflorées,
Et quoique mortes aux chansons,
Après encore à la curée.
Mais les yeux d'une âme qui s'est bel et bien cloîtrée.

Enfin; voici qu'elle m'honore de ses confidences.
J'en souffre plus qu'elle ne pense.

– «Mais, chère perdue, comment votre esprit éclairé
«Et le stylet d'acier de vos yeux infaillibles,
«N'ont-ils pas su percer à jour la mise en frais
«De cet économique et passager bellâtre?»

(VIII)

Legend

Heraldic insignia
Of anaemia! psaltery
Of autumn! I hereby consecrate with whatever
Talents and happiness my most sacred vessel
Contains this wafer of womanhood, currently afflicted by a little,
Malign, dry cough – and whom, on empty days, unknown, cloaked
In ashy greys redolent of approaching
Winter, one observes fleeing the super-human cries of the sea.

All-consuming *amours – a-gain*?

Whatever . . . these
Unvirginal lips are ready for use, already
Used, unmoved by the delights of song but eager
As hounds for a hare . . . the eyes
Meanwhile declare: "*Interdit* – no access to my cloistered soul."

So … eventually she *does* confide in me – and this
Causes me more grief than she could ever guess.

"My dear ruined maid! – how on earth
Could your gimlet eyes and razor-sharp mind
Not have seen through this fop – this mean-
Spirited lothario, who clearly spied in you a bargain!"

– «Il vint le premier; j'étais seule prés de l'âtre;
«Son cheval attaché à la grille
«Hennissait en désespéré . . .»

– «C'est touchant (pauvre fille)
«Et puis après?
«Oh! regardez, là-bas, cet épilogue sous couleur de couchant!
«Et puis, vrai,
«Remarquez que dés l'automne, l'automne!
«Les casinos,
«Qu'on abandonne
«Remisent leur piano;
«Hier l'orchestre attaqua
«Sa dernière polka,
«Hier, la dernière fanfare
«Sanglotait vers les gares . . .»

(Oh! comme elle est maigrie!
Que va-t-elle devenir?
Durcissez, durcissez,
Vous, caillots de souvenirs!)

– «Allons, les poteaux télégraphiques
«Dans les grisailles de l'exil
«Vous serviront de pleureuses de funérailles;
«Moi, c'est la saison qui veut que je m'en aille,
«Voici l'hiver qui vient.
«Ainsi soit-il.
«Ah! soignez-vous! Portez-vous bien.
«Assez! assez!

"He got to me first . . . I was at home
And alone … hitched to the gate, his horse
Whinnied in despair . . ."

"I'm moved, *ma pauvre* –
But what's new? . . .
Look there! the sun
Sets, its own epilogue, and think
Of autumn too, and how
Things change in autumn . . .
Casinos empty, their pianos
Are put away . . . yesterday
The orchestra launched
Into its last polka of the season . . . and yesterday
The railway stations harkened to a final
Sobbing fanfare . . ."

(How thin she is – what *will*
Become of her?
O curds of memory – coagulate
Coagulate!)

"Let's go – in the murk
Of exile the telegraph poles will seem
Like mourners weeping at a funeral. The coming
Winter is urging
Me to stir
And be off . . . so it goes –
Take care."
"Enough! Enough!"

«C'est toi qui as commencé!
«Tais-toi! Vos moindres clins d'yeux sont des parjures.
«Laisse! Avec vous autres rien ne dure.
«Va, je te l'assure,
«Si je t'aimais, ce serait par gageure.

«Tais-toi! tais-toi!
«On n'aime qu'une fois!»

Ah! voici que l'on compte enfin avec Moi!

Ah! ce n'est plus l'automne, alors
Ce n'est plus l'exil,
C'est la douceur des légendes, de l'âge d'or,
Des légendes des Antigones,
Douceur qui fait qu'on se demande:
«Quand donc cela se passait-il?»

C'est des légendes, c'est des gammes perlées,
Qu'on m'a tout enfant enseignées,
Oh! rien, vous dis-je, des estampes,
Les bêtes de la terre et les oiseaux du ciel
Enguirlandant les majuscules d'un Missel,
Il n'y a pas là tant de quoi saigner?

Saigner! moi pétri du plus pur limon de Cybèle!
Moi qui lui eusse été dans tout l'art des Adams
Des Édens aussi hyperboliquement fidèle
Que l'est le soleil chaque soir envers l'Occident! . . .

"You started it!"
"Be quiet – every blink of your eye
Is a betrayal. All is fleeting for you
And your type.
In fact, only to win a wager
Would I make love to you!"

"SHUT THE . . .! one loves
But *once*!"

(All this shows I am NOT to be taken for granted!)

It is autumn no more, and our exile
Is over. What comfort
Can be found in legends like those
Of the Golden Age, of characters
Like Antigone – sweet legends that have one pondering
How long ago such things were.

Legends, and the rippling scales
I was taught as a child
And engravings, and the birds
And animals enwreathing capital letters
In a prayer book – these are trifles,
Harmless, unable to draw blood, or make me

Bleed. Fashioned from the same clay as the Great
Goddess Cybele, I would have been
As faithful to her as Adam was to Eve
In Paradise, as the setting sun, each evening, is to the west.

(IX)

Oh! qu'une, d'Elle-même, un beau soir, sût venir
Ne voyant plus que boire à mes lèvres, où mourir! . . .

Oh! Baptême!
Oh! baptême de ma Raison d'être!
Faire naître un «Je t'aime!»
Et qu'il vienne à travers les hommes et les dieux,
Sous ma fenêtre,
Baissant les yeux!

Qu'il vienne, comme à l'aimant la foudre,
Et dans mon ciel d'orage qui craque et qui s'ouvre,
Et alors, les averses lustrales jusqu'au matin,
Le grand clapissement des averses toute la nuit! Enfin!

Qu'Elle vienne! et, baissant les yeux
Et s'essuyant les pieds
Au seuil de notre église, ô mes aïeux
Ministres de la Pitié,
Elle dise:

«Pour moi, tu n'es pas comme les autres hommes,
«Ils sont ces messieurs, toi tu viens des cieux.
«Ta bouche me fait baisser les yeux
«Et ton port me transporte
«Et je m'en découvre des trésors!

(IX)

If only, one fine evening, of her own
Accord, she would come to me, driven
By the urge either to drink deep at my lips – or to die!

Oh baptism,
Baptism of my raison d'être!
To give birth to a "*Je t'aime*" – in defiance
Of men and gods, arriving, eyes
Lowered, at *my*
Window! . . .

ME, irresistible as a magnet, as lightning . . . my stormy sky
Would split apart, and thunderous showers – at last! – pour down
Upon me, from midnight
Until dawn.

I see her now, eyes down, wiping
Her feet at the threshold
Of our sanctum – have pity on me
Holy ancestors! – then declaring:

"You are not like other men, like Monsieur
This or Monsieur That . . . No, to me you are heaven-sent!

"Your mouth has me dropping my gaze, and your gait
Transfigures me! Treasure

«Et je sais parfaitement que ma destinée se borne
«(Oh, j'y suis déjà bien habituée!)
«A te suivre jusqu'à ce que tu te retournes,
«Et alors t'exprimer comment tu es!

«Vraiment je ne songe pas au reste; j'attendrai
«Dans l'attendrissement de ma vie faite exprès.

«Que je te dise seulement que depuis des nuits je pleure,
«Et que mes sœurs ont bien peur que je n'en meure.

«Je pleure dans les coins, je n'ai plus goût à rien;
«Oh, j'ai tant pleuré dimanche dans mon paroissien!

«Tu me demandes pourquoi toi et non un autre,
«Ah, laisse, c'est bien toi et non un autre.

«J'en suis sûre comme du vide insensé de mon cœur
«Et comme de votre air mortellement moqueur.»

Ainsi, elle viendrait, évadée, demi-morte,
Se rouler sur le paillasson que j'ai mis à cet effet devant ma porte.
Ainsi, elle viendrait à Moi avec des yeux absolument fous,
Et elle me suivrait avec ces yeux-là partout, partout!

Upon treasure . . . Ah! my fate – and I embrace it
Already – is to follow and follow until, one day turning
Around, you find your true self
Expressed by me . . .

"Believe me, I dream of nothing but waiting for a life
Perfectly attuned to yours.

"Each night I wail, and weep
So copiously, my sisters fear the worst.

"On Sundays my tears drown my prayer-book; and
On weekdays, spurning life, curled up in any old nook
Or cranny, I cry my eyes out.

"Now don't ask why I alighted on you – I just did! For I am
as sure
That we should be together as I am of the clammy cold
Invading my heart, and of your
Look of fatal mockery . . ."

Thus she'd come, on the run, and barely
Alive, to writhe on the mat placed for exactly that purpose
Outside my door. Yes, thus
She'd come, with crazed eyes, and with those
Crazed eyes she'd follow me everywhere, everywhere . . .

(X)

Ô géraniums diaphanes, guerroyeurs sortilèges,
Sacrilèges monomanes!
Emballages, dévergondages, douches! Ô pressoirs
Des vendanges des grands soirs!
Layettes aux abois,
Thyrses au fond des bois!
Transfusions, représailles,
Relevailles, compresses et l'éternelle potion,
Angelus! n'en pouvoir plus
De débâcles nuptiales! de débâcles nuptiales! . . .

Et puis, ô mes amours,
A moi, son tous les jours,
Ô ma petite mienne, ô ma quotidienne,
Dans mon petit intérieur,
C'est-à-dire plus jamais ailleurs!

Ô ma petite quotidienne! . . .

Et quoi encore? Oh du génie,
Improvisations aux insomnies!

Et puis? L'observer dans le monde,
Et songer dans les coins:
«Oh, qu'elle est loin! Oh, qu'elle est belle!
«Oh! qui est-elle? A qui est-elle?

(X)

Diaphanous geraniums, warring
Witchery, profane bouts of monomania!
Pack-pack-packaging, extravagance, and drenchings – and grand
Grape-pressing-harvesting-evenings . . . Layettes
At bay and thyrsi buried
Deep in distant glades . . . Transfusions,
Retaliations, churchings, surgical
Dressings, potion after potion –
The *Angelus!* . . . and feeling bad, so very bad, about nuptial
Debacles . . .

And now to my own
Affairs, to my own
Mignonne, whose days are mine, all mine, for she belongs
To the quotidian, to the everyday, to my little nest indoors, for we
Never go out, do we, my dreamy
Petite quotidienne? . . .

What next? Well, here's to genius! or at least to making up
Stuff during sleep-free nights . . . don't

Stop . . . So, watching her
At some party, I retreat and ponder: "Hmm, she's
Remote and ravishing, but who is she, I wonder, and is she

«Oh, quelle inconnue! Oh, lui parler! Oh, l'emmener!»
(Et, en effet, à la fin du bal,
Elle me suivrait d'un air tout simplement fatal.)

Et puis l'éviter des semaines
Après lui avoir fait de la peine,
Et lui donner des rendez-vous
Et nous refaire un chez nous.

Et puis, la perdre des mois et des mois,
A ne plus reconnaître sa voix! . . .

Oui, le Temps salit tout,
Mais, hélas! sans en venir à bout.

Hélas! hélas! et plus la faculté d'errer,
Hypocondrie et pluie,
Et seul sous les vieux cieux,
De me faire le fou,
Le fou sans feux ni lieux
(Le pauvre, pauvre fou sans amours!)
Pour, alors, tomber bien bas
A me purifier la chair,
Et exulter au petit jour
En me fuyant en chemin de fer,
Ô Belles-Lettres, ô Beaux-Arts
Ainsi qu'un Ange à part!

Free? – who knows? O mysterious stranger, how I'd like
To talk with you! to leave with you!" (And indeed, as if I
Were her man of destiny, at the party's end
She would simply follow me . . .)

And this is how it unfolds – somehow, I hurt her feelings and have
To avoid her for weeks on end . . . then we
Meet up and we make up and we meet up, and *heigh ho!* we
Are a *we* again.

Then it's over for months and months – I can't
Even recall the sound of her voice.

Time stains
Everything yet remains
Open-ended . . .

So – alas, alack – we'll go
No more a roving . . . rain, and feeling ill
When I'm not, and finding
Myself alone under ancient skies, and playing
The fool, the homeless
Loveless, pitiful
Fool, tumbling tumbling in hope
Of cleansing this too
Too sullied flesh . . . dawn
Ecstasy and fleeing
Myself by train . . . O angelic arts, you incarnate
For me a realm above, apart.

J'aurai passé ma vie le long des quais
A faillir m'embarquer
Dans de bien funestes histoires,
Tout cela pour l'amour
De mon cœur fou de la gloire d'amour.

Oh, qu'ils sont pittoresques les trains manqués! . . .

Oh, qu'ils sont «A bientôt! à bientôt!»
Les bateaux
Du bout de la jetée! . . .

De la jetée bien charpentée
Contre la mer,
Comme ma chair
Contre l'amour.

So I'll end up dithering my life away
On dreary station platforms
Failing to embark
On sad stories, my heart lured on
Again and again
By love.

How very picturesque missed trains can be!

And boats at the end of jetties sighing
A bientôt.

Jetty – firmly built
To withstand the waves
As my flesh
Repels
Love.

(XI)

Sur une défunte

Vous ne m'aimeriez pas, voyons,
Vous ne m'aimeriez pas plus,
Pas plus, entre nous,
Qu'une fraternelle occasion? . . .
– Ah! elle ne m'aime pas!
Ah! elle ne ferait pas le premier pas
Pour que nous tombions ensemble à genoux!

Si elle avait rencontré seulement
A, B, C ou D, au lieu de Moi,
Elle les eût aimés uniquement!

Je les vois, je les vois . . .

Attendez! Je la vois
Avec les nobles A, B, C ou D.
Elle était née pour chacun d'eux.
C'est lui, Lui, quel qu'il soit,
Elle le reflète;
D'un air parfait, elle secoue la tête
Et dit que rien, rien ne peut lui déraciner
Cette étonnante destinée.

(XI)

On an Ex

You love me not
You say, *c'est fini*: yet we
Must remain friends, you add,
Best buddies.

– So be it . . . Clearly, she
Will not initiate a scene in which, together, we
Sink in rapture to our knees.

If only she had met A, B,
C or D instead of me, how devoted she
Would have been to said A, B, C or D.

I see them, I see them . . .

Listen! When I
Spy with my
Little eye, her with various nobles, I recognize that she
Was born to be with Sirs A, B,
C or D more or less equally; and whichever of these
Gets chosen, well, she
Will be his mirror, and will shake her head
O flawlessly, and declare that she
Will never be uprooted, like a weed, from her glorious destiny.

C'est Lui; elle lui dit:
«Oh, tes yeux, ta démarche!
«Oh, le son fatal de ta voix!
«Voilà si longtemps que je te cherche!
«Oh, c'est bien Toi, cette fois! . . .

Il baisse un peu sa bonne lampe,
Il la ploie, Elle, vers son cœur,
Il la baise à la tempe
Et à la place de son orphelin cœur.

Il l'endort avec des caresses tristes,
Il l'apitoie avec de petites plaintes,
Il a des considérations fatalistes,
Il prend à témoin tout ce qui existe;
Et puis, voici que l'heure tinte.

Pendant que je suis dehors,
A errer, avec elle au cœur,
A m'étonner peut-être
De l'obscurité de sa fenêtre.

Elle est chez lui, et s'y sent chez elle,
Et, comme on vient de le voir,
Elle l'aime, éperdument fidèle,
Dans toute sa beauté des soirs! . . .

Je les ai vus! Oh, ce fut trop complet!
Elle avait l'air trop fidèle
Avec ses grands yeux tout en reflets
Dans sa figure toute nouvelle!

Now here He is, and she
Says, "Your eyes are just right
For me, and the way you walk! and the way you talk! – at long
Last this time it's really You."

At which he dims his fine fine lamp
A little, and leans
Her towards him, planting kisses
In her orphaned heart, on her temple . . .

And caressing her sadly, he soothes
Her to sleep, or arouses
Her pity with his woes, or wheels out –
God help us! – his all-
Embracing philosophy until suddenly
Hark! It's late! Ay mi! The hour sounds! . . .

Meanwhile, outside, brooding
On her, I find
Myself beneath her darkened window, and wonder
At it . . .

How at home she feels
Chez lui! . . . The evidence mounts up – she loves him – will be
Madly faithful to him will lavish
Her crepuscular beauty on him, not me.

I have seen them together and, dearie me, how
Consummately she exudes
Fidelity, her eyes aglow, her face

Et je ne serais qu'un pis-aller,

Et je ne serais qu'un pis-aller,
Comme l'est mon jour dans le Temps,
Comme l'est ma place dans l'Espace;
Et l'on ne voudrait pas que je m'accommodasse
De ce sort vraiment dégoûtant! . . .

Non, non! pour Elle, tout ou rien!
Et je m'en irai donc comme un fou,
A travers l'automne qui vient,
Dans le grand vent où il y a tout!

Je me dirai: Oh! à cette heure,
Elle est bien loin, elle pleure,
Le grand vent se lamente aussi,
Et moi je suis seul dans ma demeure,
Avec mon noble cœur tout transi,
Et sans amour et sans personne,
Car tout est misère, tout est automne,
Tout est endurci et sans merci.

Et, si je t'avais aimée ainsi,
Tu l'aurais trouvée trop bien bonne! Merci!

Unrecognizable.

Lover of last resort –

Lover of last resort –
That's me, floating
Through time and space . . . and would you
Have me accept a life compounded
Of dishonour and disgrace?

No, in thunder! It's do
Or die – oh see me charge, like a madman,
Into the very teeth of autumn, into the wind
In which everything whirls!

– Right now, I
Soliloquize, she's weeping far
Away, and the wind
Is weeping too, and I'm alone
In my abode, chilled and love-sick
To the bone, and there's no
One here but suffering
And indifference and autumn.

"*Oh pull the other one . . . thanks but NO*
Thanks" – that's surely how
You would have responded had I
Declared myself so.

(XII)

Get thee to a nunnery: why wouldst thou be a breeder of sinners? I am myself indifferent honest; but yet I could accuse me of such things, that it were better my mother had not borne me. We are arrant knaves, all; believe none of us. Go thy ways to a nunnery

HAMLET

Noire bise, averse glapissante,
Et fleuve noir, et maisons closes,
Et quartiers sinistres comme des Morgues,
Et l'Attardé qui à la remorque traîne
Toute la misère du cœur et des choses,
Et la souillure des innocentes qui traînent,
Et crie à l'averse. «Oh, arrose, arrose
«Mon cœur si brûlant, ma chair si intéressante!»

Oh, elle, mon cœur et ma chair, que fait-elle? . . .

Oh! si elle est dehors par ce vilain temps,
De quelles histoires trop humaines rentre-t-elle?
Et si elle est dedans,
A ne pas pouvoir dormir par ce grand vent,
Pense-t-elle au Bonheur,
Au bonheur à tout prix
Disant: tout plutôt que mon cœur reste ainsi incompris?

(XII)

Get thee to a nunnery: why wouldst thou be a breeder of sinners? I am myself indifferent honest; but yet I could accuse me of such things, that it were better my mother had not borne me. We are arrant knaves, all: believe none of us. Go thy ways to a nunnery.

HAMLET

Dark winter wind, yowling
Torrents of rain, a pitch-black river beneath shuttered
Houses, *quartiers* creepy as mortuaries, through which a late-
Night wanderer drags his gloom, brooding
On girls, once innocent, now dawdling, adrift
In the storm: "Oh drench," he cries
To the weather, "this flaming heart, and drench
My burning heart, my fascinating flesh."

My heart, *my* flesh, *her* – where, what, where
Is she? Could she be out
And about in *this*, on her way
Back from . . . from what people get up to?
Or if she's inside, kept
Awake by the storm, could she be thinking happy thoughts
  about, say,
Happiness, or is she musing, "I can cope with anything, but hate
Being misunderstood?"

Soigne-toi, soigne-toi! pauvre cœur aux abois.

(Langueurs, débilité, palpitations, larmes,
Oh, cette misère de vouloir être notre femme!)

Ô pays, ô famille!
Et l'âme toute tournée
D'héroïques destinées
Au-delà des saintes vieilles filles,
Et pour cette année!

Nuit noire, maisons closes, grand vent,
Oh, dans un couvent, dans un couvent!

Un couvent dans ma ville natale
Douce de vingt-mille âmes à peine,
Entre le lycée et la préfecture
Et vis-à-vis la cathédrale,
Avec ces anonymes en robes grises,
Dans la prière, le ménage, les travaux de couture;
Et que cela suffise . . .
Et méprise sans envie
Tout ce qui n'est pas cette vie de Vestale
Provinciale,
Et marche à jamais glacée,
Les yeux baissés.

Oh! je ne puis voir ta petite scène fatale à vif,
Et ton pauvre air dans ce huis-clos,

Take care, take care, poor heart
At bay.

(Fainting fits, palpitations, lassitude, and tears – how
Truly ghastly to want to be my wife!)

O my land and
O my family – the soul
Stirs at heroics, at destinies beyond the dreams
Of God-fearing spinsters, all
Done and dusted this very year.

Black night, shuttered houses, fearsome
Winds – to a nunnery, go, to a nunnery!

To a nunnery in the place where I grew up, a town
That boasts some twenty thousand souls . . .
Across from the cathedral, between
The lycée and the prefecture, are nameless, grey-robed women
Praying, cleaning, plying
Their needles – *ça suffit,*
N'est-ce pas? Eyes down, body
Glacial, scorn all
Unbecoming a provincial
Maiden . . .

Ach, how I flinch
At the thought of you cloistered, impoverished, attempting bleak

Et tes tristes petits gestes instinctifs,
Et peut-être incapable de sanglots!

Oh! ce ne fut pas et ce ne peut être,
Oh! tu n'es pas comme les autres,
Crispées aux rideaux de leur fenêtre
Devant le soleil couchant qui dans son sang se vautre!
Oh! tu n'as pas l'âge,
Oh, dis, tu n'auras jamais l'âge,
Oh, tu me promets de rester sage comme une image? . . .

La nuit est à jamais noire,
Le vent est grandement triste,
Tout dit la vieille histoire
Qu'il faut être deux au coin du feu,
Tout bâcle un hymne fataliste,
Mais toi, il ne faut pas que tu t'abandonnes,
A ces vilains jeux! . . .

A ces grandes pitiés du mois de novembre!
Reste dans ta petite chambre,
Passe, à jamais glacée,
Tes beaux yeux irréconciliablement baissés.

Oh, qu'elle est là-bas, que la nuit est noire!
Que la vie est une étourdissante foire!
Que toutes sont créature, et que tout est routine!

Oh, que nous mourrons!

Little gestures, too drained even
To cry.

Such scenes weren't and won't
Be . . . it's others, not you, who must clench the curtains framing
A sun as it gorily sets
In its own blood. You are too young, and must remain
Young, and promise
To stay as good, like a child,
As gold.

Night black and endless, and the grief-
Stricken winds have me yearning for a little
Fairy-tale bliss, beside the fire, with my beloved . . . alluring,
Ill-fitting, inevitable – but *you*
Must never collapse, become merely convention's
Hideous plaything.

Remember, and resist the sorrows
Of November – don't even leave your little room, or if you must
Go out, act all frostily, and keep
Your eyes, your magnificent eyes lowered, veiled.

Her and black night, out there, and life
A bewildering carnival, at once a rut and a bodily
Affair.

Ach – that we shall die!

Eh bien, pour aimer ce qu'il y a d'histoires
Derrière ces beaux yeux d'orpheline héroïne,
Ô Nature, donne-moi la force et le courage
De me croire en âge,
Ô Nature relève-moi le front!
Puisque, tôt ou tard, nous mourrons . . .

And so, to love what lurks
Behind our orphan heroine's fabulous eyes
I need, O Nature, strength
And courage to trust what the years
Have made of me . . . to look up, clear . . .

Ach – later, or sooner, we shall die . . .

OTHER TITLES FROM THE SONG CAVE:

1. *A Dark Dreambox of Another Kind* by **Alfred Starr Hamilton**
2. *My Enemies* by **Jane Gregory**
3. *Rude Woods* by **Nate Klug**
4. *Georges Braque and Others* by **Trevor Winkfield**
5. *The Living Method* by **Sara Nicholson**
6. *Splash State* by **Todd Colby**
7. *Essay Stanzas* by **Thomas Meyer**
8. *Illustrated Games of Patience* by **Ben Estes**
9. *Dark Green* by **Emily Hunt**
10. *Honest James* by **Christian Schlegel**
11. *M* by **Hannah Brooks-Motl**
12. *What the Lyric Is* by **Sara Nicholson**
13. *The Hermit* by **Lucy Ives**
14. *The Orchid Stories* by **Kenward Elmslie**
15. *Do Not Be a Gentleman When You Say Goodnight* by **Mitch Sisskind**
16. *HAIRDO* by **Rachel B. Glaser**
17. *Motor Maids across the Continent* by **Ron Padgett**
18. *Songs for Schizoid Siblings* by **Lionel Ziprin**
19. *Professionals of Hope: The Selected Writings of* **Subcomandante Marcos**
20. *Fort Not* by **Emily Skillings**
21. *Riddles, Etc.* by **Geoffrey Hilsabeck**
22. *CHARAS: The Improbable Dome Builders* by **Syeus Mottel** (Co-published with Pioneer Works)
23. *YEAH NO* by **Jane Gregory**
24. *Nioque of the Early-Spring* by **Francis Ponge**
25. *Smudgy and Lossy* by **John Myers**
26. *The Desert* by **Brandon Shimoda**
27. *Scardanelli* by **Friederike Mayröcker**

28. *The Alley of Fireflies and Other Stories* by **Raymond Roussel**
29. *CHANGES: Notes on Choreography* by **Merce Cunningham** (Co-published with the Merce Cunningham Trust)
30. *My Mother Laughs* by **Chantal Akerman**
31. *Earth* by **Hannah Brooks-Motl**
32. *Everything and Other Poems* by **Charles North**
33. *Paper Bells* by **Phan Nhiên Hạo**
34. *Photographs: Together & Alone* by **Karlheinz Weinberger**
35. *A Better Place Is Hard to Find* by **Aaron Fagan**
36. *Rough Song* by **Blanca Varela**
37. *In the Same Light: 200 Poems for Our Century From the Migrants & Exiles of the Tang Dynasty,* translated by **Wong May**
38. *On the Mesa: An Anthology of Bolinas Writing (50th Anniversary Edition),* edited by **Ben Estes and Joel Weishaus**
39. *Listen My Friend, This Is the Dream I Dreamed Last Night* by **Cody-Rose Clevidence**
40. *Poetries* by **Georges Schehadé**
41. *Wings in Time* by **Callie Garnett**
42. *Two Murals* by **Jesús Castillo**
43. *Punks: New & Selected Poems* by **John Keene**
44. *ABC Moonlight* by **Ben Estes**
45. *Star Lake* by **Arda Collins**
46. *The Maybe-Bird* by **Jennifer Elise Foerster**
47. *Seriously Well* by **Helge Torvund**
48. *Dereliction* by **Gabrielle Octavia Rucker**
49. *Bookworm: Conversations with* **Michael Silverblatt**
50. *April* by **Sara Nicholson**
51. *Valley of the Many-Colored Grasses* by **Ronald Johnson**
52. *The Sphinx and the Milky Way: Selections from the Notebooks of* **Charles Burchfield**
53. *Telling the Truth as It Comes Up: Selected Talks & Essays 1991-2018* by **Alice Notley**